SPECTRUM®

REPRODUCIBLE

Test Practice

With Free Online Resources for each U.S. State

GRADE 5

Published by Spectrum®
an imprint of Carson-Dellosa Publishing LLC
Greensboro, NC

W9-ALV-882

Spectrum®
An imprint of Carson-Dellosa Publishing LLC
P.O. Box 35665
Greensboro, NC 27425 USA

Printed in the U.S.A. • All rights reserved.   ISBN: 978-1-62057-597-0

02-343137784

The Common Core State Standards

What Are the Standards?

The Common Core State Standards have been adopted by most U.S. states. They were developed by a state-led initiative to make sure all students are prepared for success in college and in the global, twenty-first century workforce. They provide a clear understanding of what students are expected to learn in English language arts and mathematics.

These new learning standards for your child are:

- Rigorous.

- Based on the best available evidence and research.

- Aligned with college and work expectations.

- Benchmarked to the highest educational standards from around the world.

What Do the English Language Arts Standards Mean for My Student?

In grade 5, English language arts standards focus on reading, writing, speaking and listening, and language skills (grammar and usage).

These standards set expectations for what it means to be a skilled reader and writer in the twenty-first century. They provide strategies for reading fiction and nonfiction closely and attentively. They help students look for evidence and make critical judgments about the vast amount of print and digital information available.

What Do the Mathematics Standards Mean for My Student?

Examples of grade 5 mathematics standards include fractions (adding and subtracting fractions) and measurement and data (finding the volume of three-dimensional shapes).

These standards increase the depth and focus of math topics studied in each grade. Instead of sampling a wide variety of skills each year, students work to develop deep understanding and mastery of a few concepts.

Free Online State-Specific Test Practice

For additional **free** *Spectrum Test Practice* resources customized to your child's grade level and the U.S. state where you live, follow these instructions:

1. Go to:

   carsondellosa.com/spectrum

2. Click on *Spectrum Test Practice Free Online Materials* and register to download your free practice pages.

3. Download and print PDF pages customized for your state and your child's grade level.

Online Features Include:

- Links to Common Core State Standards information for your state

- A comprehensive practice test aligned to Common Core English language arts and mathematics standards for your child's grade level

- State-specific test items within the practice test, designated by this symbol: **1.**

  These items are aligned to the unique standards that have been adopted by your state in addition to Common Core State Standards.

- An answer key for practice test pages

How to Use This Book

Time spent practicing for standardized tests will benefit your child greatly. With the adoption of Common Core State Standards by most U.S. states, educators are relying more than ever on test results to compare your child's progress with that of others around the nation and the world. The resources in this book will help ease anxieties and prepare your child for test day.

What's Inside?

- **Lesson pages** contain sample questions and examples related to a specific skill. The assumption is that your student has received prior instruction on the topics. These pages can provide focused practice.

- **Sample tests** are shorter tests with questions about one subtopic.

- **Practice tests** are comprehensive tests with questions about the entire content area.

Practice Options

Choose how you will use the materials to meet the needs of your student.

- Select pages matching the skills your student needs to practice most.

- Assign lesson pages for practice throughout the week. End the week with a sample or practice test related to those skills.

- Administer a timed practice test in a quiet setting. For a fifth grade student, allow 1.25 minutes per question. After the test, check answers together and talk about what was most difficult.

Test-Taking  Clues

- Look for the symbol shown above throughout the book. Talk about the clues with your child.

- Read and review directions and examples. Talk about how test questions look and point out words and phrases that often appear in directions.

- Skip difficult questions, returning to them if time allows.

- Guess at questions you do not know.

- Answer all the questions.

- Try to stay relaxed and approach the test with confidence!

Name _____   Date _____

● **Lesson 1: Synonyms**

Directions: Read each item. Fill in the circle next to the word that means the same or about the same as the underlined word.

9/10

Examples

A.   a small dwelling

- Ⓐ school
- ⬤Ⓑ home
- Ⓒ suburb
- Ⓓ tribe

B.   Fascinating means —

- Ⓕ disturbing
- Ⓖ annoying
- ⓗ pleasant
- Ⓙ interesting

 Clue Choose only one answer. Be sure to fill in the circle completely.

● **Practice**

1.   **successful corporation**
- Ⓐ business
- Ⓑ team
- Ⓒ person
- Ⓓ country

2.   **skilled laborer**
- Ⓕ musician
- Ⓖ professor
- ⓗ worker
- Ⓙ relative

3.   **tiny particle**
- Ⓐ animal
- Ⓑ package
- Ⓒ piece
- Ⓓ gift

4.   **a desert region**
- Ⓔ area
- Ⓖ culture
- Ⓗ religion
- Ⓙ plant

5.   **An imaginary story is —**
- Ⓐ biographical
- Ⓑ fictional
- Ⓒ actual
- Ⓓ humorous

6.   **To interpret is to —**
- Ⓕ organize
- Ⓖ adjust
- Ⓗ catch
- Ⓙ explain

7.   **To pave is to —**
- Ⓐ cover
- Ⓑ hide
- Ⓒ recycle
- Ⓓ fly

8.   **An affectionate person is —**
- Ⓕ hostile
- Ⓖ adorable
- ⓗ loving
- Ⓙ ill

STOP

READING: VOCABULARY

● Lesson 2: Vocabulary Skills

Directions: Read each item. Fill in the circle next to the word that means the same or about the same as the underlined word.

Examples

A. <u>admire</u> a leader
- Ⓐ advise
- Ⓑ detest
- Ⓒ trust
- Ⓓ respect

B. A <u>journalist</u> interviewed the athlete. Journalist means —
- Ⓕ referee
- Ⓖ reporter
- Ⓗ collector
- Ⓙ scientist

If you are not sure which answer is correct, take your best guess. Eliminate answer choices you know are wrong.

● Practice

1. Complete the <u>assignment</u>.
   - Ⓐ task
   - Ⓑ assistant
   - Ⓒ design
   - Ⓓ office

2. <u>Focus</u> your attention.
   - Ⓕ fluctuate
   - Ⓖ irritate
   - Ⓗ compile
   - Ⓙ concentrate

3. good <u>publicity</u>
   - Ⓐ appreciation
   - Ⓑ public attention
   - Ⓒ publisher
   - Ⓓ celebrity

4. Tom waited <u>anxiously</u> for the announcement. Anxiously means —
   - Ⓕ nervously
   - Ⓖ without concern
   - Ⓗ quickly
   - Ⓙ with anger

5. The story was about children who <u>benefit</u> from the fundraiser. Benefit means —
   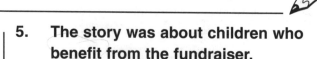
   - Ⓐ to volunteer
   - Ⓑ to serve
   - Ⓒ to raise money
   - Ⓓ to receive help

6. Her hard work was <u>complimented</u>. Complimented means —
   - Ⓕ disliked
   - Ⓖ given away freely
   - Ⓗ praised
   - Ⓙ completed

7. The workers went on <u>strike</u>. Strike means —
   - Ⓐ to take a vacation
   - Ⓑ to hit
   - Ⓒ to stop working in order to protest
   - Ⓓ to throw a ball

STOP

READING: VOCABULARY

● Lesson 3: Antonyms

Directions: Read each item. Fill in the circle next to the word that means the opposite of the underlined word.

8/10

Examples

A.   departed guests
- (A) honored
- (B) excited
- (C) gathered ✓
- (D) neglected

B.   rare appearances
- (F) frequent
- (G) old ✓
- (H) uncommon
- (J) distant

Clue Read each item carefully. Choose the answer that means the opposite.

● Practice

1.   Accept the truth.
- (A) deny
- (B) understand
- (C) illustrate
- (D) respect

2.   attentive people
- (F) beautiful
- (G) prosperous
- (H) messy
- (J) heedless

3.   an absurd story
- (A) logical
- (B) exciting
- (C) rewarding
- (D) fanciful

4.   generous servings
- (F) large
- (G) grateful
- (H) small
- (J) general

5.   brief description
- (A) important
- (B) lengthy
- (C) short
- (D) casual

6.   employ the workers
- (F) befriend
- (G) manage
- (H) argue with
- (J) dismiss

7.   confident in your abilities
- (A) uncertain
- (B) assured
- (C) proud
- (D) neglectful

8.   superior attitude
- (F) extreme
- (G) inferior
- (H) great
- (J) focused

STOP

READING: VOCABULARY

● Lesson 4: Multi-Meaning Words

Directions: Read each item. Fill in the circle next to the answer you think is correct.

Examples

A. Unemployment is <u>running</u> high here since the factory closed.

In which sentence does the word <u>running</u> mean the same thing as in the sentence above?

- (A) Tracy saw the horse <u>running</u> through the field. ✓
- (B) Beth was <u>running</u> the lawn mower.
- (C) Club attendance was <u>running</u> low due to heavy snow.
- (D) Peter is <u>running</u> for class president.

B. Choose the word that fits in both the blanks.

Set the package __off__ to the side.
We had the day __off__.

- (F) over
- (G) off
- (H) apart
- (J) away

Clue Read the question carefully. Use the meaning of the sentences to help you choose the right answer.

● Practice

1. Groaning, he rolled over and <u>planted</u> his feet firmly on the floor.

In which sentence does the word <u>planted</u> mean the same thing as in the sentence above?

- (A) Jean <u>planted</u> four rows of cucumbers.
- (B) The lawyer claimed that the evidence had been <u>planted</u>. ✓
- (C) The settlers <u>planted</u> new crops.
- (D) Jo <u>planted</u> her feet in the dirt before swinging the bat.

2. Barb put a clean __cover__ on the bed.

Jason washed the cookie __cover__ after he finished baking.

- (F) pillow
- (G) tray
- (H) sheet
- (J) cover

3. We __Drew__ nearer to the warmth of the campfire.

He __Drew__ the wrong conclusion from the facts that were presented.

- (A) drew
- (B) moved
- (C) identified
- (D) illustrated

STOP

READING: VOCABULARY

● Lesson 5: Words in Context

Directions: Read the paragraph. Find the word below that fits best in each numbered blank.

Examples

The United States Capitol is well known for its ___(A)___, or round room. The room has a large dome. A bronze Statue of Freedom ___(B)___ on top of the dome.

A.
- (A) parlor
- (B) library
- (C) rotunda
- (D) media center

B.
- (F) stands
- (G) centered
- (H) flies
- (J) bends

Clue Look carefully at each answer. Choose the word that sounds best in the sentence.

● Practice

The Montgolfier brothers ___(1)___ the hot-air balloon in 1783. However, they ___(2)___ never guessed how high or how far one of these balloons could go. In the brothers' first ___(3)___, they used a huge bag made of paper and ___(4)___. They held its open end over a ___(5)___. The bag filled with smoke and hot air. Then it rose into the air and ___(6)___ for a mile and a half.

1.
- (A) discovered
- (B) invented
- (C) explored
- (D) arranged

2.
- (F) probably
- (G) randomly
- (H) rarely
- (J) frequently

3.
- (A) grade
- (B) demonstration
- (C) hope
- (D) suggestion

4.
- (F) steel
- (G) bricks
- (H) mortar
- (J) fabric

5.
- (A) pool
- (B) puddle
- (C) fire
- (D) engine

6.
- (F) dropped
- (G) recorded
- (H) sank
- (I) floated

STOP

READING: VOCABULARY

● Lesson 6: Word Study

Directions: Read each item. Fill in the circle for the answer you think is correct.

Examples

A. Which of these words probably comes from the Latin word *albus,* meaning "white"?

- Ⓐ albino
- Ⓑ album
- ⓒ algebra
- Ⓓ alchemy

B. Margo was _____ that her team lost the game.

Which of these words would indicate that Margo felt sad?

- Ⓕ elated
- Ⓖ frustrated
- Ⓗ disappointed
- Ⓙ angry

 Clue Look for key words in the question. The key words will help you choose the right answer.

● Practice

1. Which of these words probably comes from the Greek word *demos kratos* meaning "rule of the people"?

- Ⓐ demolish
- Ⓑ democracy
- ⓒ demote
- Ⓓ demonstration

2. Which of these words probably comes from the Latin word *audire* meaning "to hear"?

- Ⓕ audit
- Ⓖ auburn
- Ⓗ auction
- Ⓙ audio

3. The stadium was filled with _____. Which of these words would indicate that there was an audience at the stadium?

- Ⓐ spectators
- Ⓑ performers
- ⓒ soldiers
- Ⓓ employees

4. Ramon's grandfather stored family _____ in the attic.

Which of these words means there were heirlooms in the attic?

- Ⓕ antiques
- Ⓖ pets
- Ⓗ chores
- Ⓙ rubbish

For numbers 5 and 6, choose the answer that best defines the underlined part.

5. <u>pre</u>cede <u>pre</u>dict

- Ⓐ after
- Ⓑ around
- ⓒ before
- Ⓓ between

6. bio<u>logy</u> geo<u>logy</u>

- Ⓕ person who
- Ⓖ study of
- Ⓗ quality of being
- Ⓙ full of

STOP

READING: VOCABULARY

● Lesson 7: Words From Greek and Latin, Idioms

Directions: Choose the answer that best defines the underlined phrase or word part.

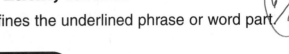

Examples

A. We want to go outside, but it is <u>raining cats and dogs</u>!

- (A) full of pet animals ✓
- (B) a beautiful day
- (C) too crowded
- (D) raining very hard

B. <u>photo</u>synthesis

- (F) plants
- (G) light
- (H) greenery
- (J) trees

● Practice

1. I didn't have any trouble with the test. **It was <u>a piece of cake</u>!**

- (A) It tasted good. ✓
- (B) It was easy.
- (C) It looked nice.
- (D) It was hard work.

2. Stop wasting time, and <u>grab the bull by the horns</u>.

- (F) Take action. ✓
- (G) Get out of the way.
- (H) Look for a new pet.
- (J) Hurry up.

3. William went to the meeting, but he felt like <u>a fish out of water</u>.

- (A) going swimming
- (B) out of place
- (C) hard to breathe
- (D) unable to make friends

4. <u>geo</u>graphy

- (F) Earth ✓
- (G) maps
- (H) rocks
- (J) science

5. <u>hemi</u>sphere

- (A) ball
- (B) round ✓
- (C) half
- (D) whole

6. <u>thermo</u>s

- (F) light
- (G) month
- (H) carry ✓
- (J) heat

STOP

Name _____ Date_____

READING: VOCABULARY
SAMPLE TEST

Directions: Read each item. Fill in the circle next to the word that means the same or about the same as the underlined word.

Examples

A. <u>spoiled</u> fruit
- (A) citrus
- (B) yellow
- (C) fresh
- (D) rotten ●

B. A <u>helper</u> is the same as an —
- (F) adviser
- (G) assistant ●
- (H) elevator
- (J) organizer

For numbers 1–13, fill in the circle next to the word that means the same or about the same as the underlined word.

1. Do it <u>now.</u>
- (A) immediately
- (B) later
- (C) soon
- (D) slowly

2. artistic <u>film</u>
- (F) play
- (G) drama
- (H) movie
- (J) episode

3. in the <u>cellar</u>
- (A) attic
- (B) basement
- (C) garage
- (D) workshop

4. newspaper <u>article</u>
- (F) story
- (G) novel
- (H) journal
- (J) book

5. Something that has <u>concluded</u> is —
- (A) in progress
- (B) continuing
- (C) beginning
- (D) finished

6. An <u>irregular</u> shape is —
- (F) symmetrical
- (G) uneven
- (H) balanced
- (J) broken

7. A <u>career</u> is —
- (A) a hobby
- (B) a university
- (C) an occupation
- (D) a library

8. To take a <u>brisk</u> walk means to walk —
- (F) quickly
- (G) leisurely
- (H) by yourself
- (J) with others

GO ON

READING: VOCABULARY
SAMPLE TEST (cont.)

9. The <u>association</u> works to help animals.
   Association means —
   - (A) occupation
   - (B) college
   - (C) friendship
   - (D) organization

10. You can see the sunlight through the <u>sheer</u> curtains.
    Sheer means —
    - (F) white
    - (G) thick
    - (H) transparent
    - (J) open

11. Helga is a <u>loyal</u> friend.
    Loyal means —
    - (A) devoted
    - (B) dangerous
    - (C) good
    - (D) dishonest

12. The timeline marked the <u>milestones</u> of the Civil War.
    Milestones means —
    - (F) speeches
    - (G) roads
    - (H) events
    - (J) condltions

13. Jacob <u>corresponded</u> with his pen pal.
    Corresponded means he —
    - (A) played
    - (B) visited
    - (C) telephoned
    - (D) wrote

For numbers 14–19, fill in the circle next to the word that means the <u>opposite</u> of the underlined word.

14. <u>express</u> your thoughts
    - (F) yell
    - (G) withhold
    - (H) summarize
    - (J) tell

15. <u>obvious</u> signs
    - (A) unclear
    - (B) apparent
    - (C) momentary
    - (D) secondary

16. <u>ignore</u> the noise
    - (F) contribute to
    - (G) notice
    - (H) overlook
    - (J) behave

17. <u>respect</u> for the law
    - (A) obedience
    - (B) trust
    - (C) honor
    - (D) contempt

18. with <u>regret</u>
    - (F) happiness
    - (G) sorrow
    - (H) fear
    - (J) bravery

19. a great <u>achievement</u>
    - (A) victory
    - (B) failure
    - (C) mistake
    - (D) accomplishment

GO ON

Name _____   Date_____

For numbers 20–23, choose the word that best completes both sentences.

20. Please _____ my coat to the bus.
An actor's voice must _____ to the last row of seats.
- (F) deliver
- (G) reach
- (H) take
- (J) carry

21. Throw the _____ to me. Sheila wore a formal dress to the _____.
- (A) party
- (B) ball
- (C) coat
- (D) dance

22. Reach out with your _____.
The soldiers gathered _____ for the battle.
- (F) arms
- (G) legs
- (H) supplies
- (J) muskets

23. The class visited a _____ art museum.
He had to pay a _____ for speeding.
- (A) modern
- (B) charge
- (C) quality
- (D) fine

For numbers 24 and 25, fill in the circle next to the answer that you think is correct.

24. I tied the key on a string.
In which sentence does the word *key* mean the same thing as in the sentence above?
- (F) The key to a riddle provides the answer.
- (G) I sailed around the key.
- (H) I opened the door with my key.
- (J) The choir sang in key.

25. I opened a savings account at the bank.
In which sentence does the word *bank* mean the same thing as in the sentence above?
- (A) The pilot flew through a bank of clouds.
- (B) My mom is a bank manager.
- (C) My house sits on the bank of a river.
- (D) Bank to the left at the intersection.

For numbers 26 and 27, choose the answer that best defines the underlined part.

26. subway   submarine
- (F) under
- (G) over
- (H) apart
- (J) backward

27. careless   thoughtless
- (A) less than one
- (B) full of
- (C) without
- (D) forward

978-1-62057-597-0 *Spectrum Test Practice 5*

READING: VOCABULARY
SAMPLE TEST (cont.)

For numbers 28–31, fill in the circle next to the correct answer.

28. Which of these words probably comes from the Latin word *barba,* meaning "beard"?

    (F) barb
    (G) barbarian
    (H) barber
    (J) bargain

29. Which of these words probably comes from the Greek word *kolla,* meaning "glue"?

    (A) college
    (B) collage
    (C) collide
    (D) collar

30. The pioneers moved west to settle the
    _____.

    Which of these words means the settlers moved to the border of their country?

    (F) soil
    (G) state
    (H) suburb
    (J) frontier

31. The police officer inspected the accident _____.

    Which of these words means the officer inspected the location of the accident?

    (A) site
    (B) situation
    (C) victims
    (D) problem

For numbers 32–35, read the paragraph. Find the word below that fits best in each numbered blank.

Wang Yani was born in a small town in southern China. Her father, an art teacher, recognized her interest and _____(32) in art very early in her life. Her first art _____(33) was held in Shanghai when Yani was only four years old. Yani paints using traditional Chinese _____(34), but her style of broad brush strokes, say her critics, is refreshingly _____(35).

32. (F) disgust
    (G) personality
    (H) talent
    (J) charm

33. (A) exhibition
    (B) experience
    (C) school
    (D) project

34. (F) containers
    (G) wood
    (H) homes
    (J) materials

35. (A) stale
    (B) unique
    (C) menacing
    (D) undeveloped

STOP

READING: COMPREHENSION

● Lesson 8: Main Idea

Directions: Read each item. Fill in the circle next to the answer you think is correct.

Example

In school, veterinarians learn about animals' bodies, animal diseases, and the medicines used to treat them. They also learn how to perform surgeries.

A. What is this passage about?

- Ⓐ how veterinarians are trained
- Ⓑ the duties of a veterinarian
- Ⓒ equipment that veterinarians use
- Ⓓ the clothing that veterinarians wear

Clue Look for a topic sentence in the passage. This will help you understand the main idea.

● Practice

An urban habitat is home to many animals. Birds like pigeons and starlings nest on tall buildings. Mice and rats build their nests in or near buildings. Squirrels, rabbits, and opossums make their homes in the wide-open spaces of city parks. Timid animals like foxes and raccoons search for food in neighborhood garbage cans at night. Perhaps the favorite city animals, though, are the ones that live in the homes of people—cats, dogs, and other animal friends we call pets.

1. **What would be a good title for this passage?**

   - Ⓐ Pests Among Us
   - Ⓑ City Critters
   - Ⓒ A Nocturnal Nuisance
   - Ⓓ An Urban Legend

2. **What is the main idea of this passage?**

   - Ⓕ People should protect city animals.
   - Ⓖ Urban animals cause many problems.
   - Ⓗ Many animals live in the city.
   - Ⓙ People who live in cities should not have pets.

3. **If the author wanted to continue describing urban habitats, what would be a good topic for the next paragraph?**

   - Ⓐ career opportunities in cities
   - Ⓑ urban crime
   - Ⓒ city schools
   - Ⓓ plants that can be found in cities

4. **What is the author's purpose for writing this passage?**

   - Ⓕ to tell people about animals that live in urban habitats
   - Ⓖ to warn people about urban animals
   - Ⓗ to present a plan to city officials about protecting animals
   - Ⓙ to explain how people and animals work together

READING: COMPREHENSION

● Lesson 9: Recalling Details

Directions: Read each item. Fill in the circle next to the answer you think is correct.

Example

People laugh when I tell them what kind of farm we have. My family raises catfish! The fish live in ponds on our farm. We feed them pellets that look almost like the food you feed cats or dogs.

A. What does the food for the catfish look like?

- (A) birdseed
- (B) dog food ✓
- (C) pebbles
- (D) sand

 Clue   Read the questions first. Then while you read the passage, you can look for the information that you will be asked about.

● Practice

Today was very busy. Jane, Carl, and I went out around 8:00 to fill our buckets with blackberries. It was hard work, and we didn't get back until it was time for lunch. This afternoon, Aunt Mara showed us how to wash and sort the berries. When it was time to make jam, Aunt Mara did the cooking part. Then she let us fill the jars and decorate the labels. Now Aunt Mara is letting me take a jar of jam home for Mom. She'll be surprised that I helped make it. I hope the rest of my stay here is as much fun as today was.

1. **What was the first thing the narrator did?**
- (A) picked blackberries ✓
- (B) ate lunch
- (C) decorated labels
- (D) washed berries

2. **Who cooked the berries?**
- (F) the narrator
- (G) Jane
- (H) Carl
- (J) Aunt Mara ✓

3. **How does the narrator feel about this experience?**
- (A) frustrated
- (B) surprised
- (C) happy
- (D) angry

4. **When did the children pick the berries?**
- (F) at night
- (G) in the afternoon
- (H) in the evening
- (J) in the morning

STOP

Name _____ Date_____

READING: COMPREHENSION

● **Lesson 10: Inferencing/Drawing Conclusions**

Directions: Read each item. Fill in the circle next to the answer you think is correct.

Example

Police officers carry equipment that helps them to protect themselves and other people. They carry guns, nightsticks, flashlights, and handcuffs on their belts. Some wear bullet-proof vests. They also carry two-way radios so they can call other officers for assistance.

A. **Why would police officers need equipment for protection?**

- (A) because they teach people about the laws
- (B) because they are trained to use the equipment
- (C) because sometimes their work can be dangerous
- (D) because they need to write reports

 Clue Look carefully at all the answer choices before you choose your answer.

● **Practice**

I was so nervous. I hadn't seen Abbie in three years, not since my mom got that new job. I remember the day we moved away. Abbie brought me our photograph in a frame. I gave her a necklace with a friendship charm on it. We promised to stay friends forever. Now that I was finally going to see her again, I wondered if we would still like the same kinds of things and laugh at the same kinds of jokes. I rubbed my sweaty palms on my jeans as we pulled into Abbie's driveway.

1. **Why hasn't the narrator seen Abbie for three years?**
   - (A) they were best friends
   - (B) because they didn't like each other's gifts
   - (C) because they had a fight
   - (D) because the narrator had to move away

2. **Why are the narrator's palms sweaty?**
   - (F) because she is nervous
   - (G) because she has a fever
   - (H) because she feels sick
   - (J) because she doesn't want to move

3. **The passage gives you enough information to believe that the narrator —**
   - (A) was angry at her mom for making her move.
   - (B) had a special friendship with Abbie.
   - (C) liked her new school.
   - (D) doesn't keep her promises.

4. **The narrator will feel happy if —**
   - (F) Abbie is not home.
   - (G) Abbie has changed a lot.
   - (H) she gets to move again.
   - (J) she and Abbie still get along.

 STOP

Name _____ Date _____

READING: COMPREHENSION

● Lesson 11: Fact and Opinion/Cause and Effect

Directions: Read each item. Fill in the circle next to the answer you think is correct.

Example

To pay off its national debts, the British government increased the taxes paid on its products by its colonists. The American colonists thought this was very unfair. They protested by throwing British tea and merchandise into Boston Harbor.

A. **Why did the American colonists throw tea into Boston Harbor?**

- Ⓐ because the British had too many debts
- ⓧ Ⓑ because they wanted coffee instead of tea
- Ⓒ because they didn't like tea
- Ⓓ because they thought the tax increase was unfair

 Clue Look for key words in the question and find the words in the passage. This will help you locate the correct answer.

● Practice

The legend of Santa Clause started with stories about a fourth-century bishop. This bishop, Nicholas, was said to be kind, generous, and fond of children. In one story, Nicholas threw a bag of coins down the chimney of a needy family. Long after his death, Nicholas was named a saint. On his saint's day in December, Dutch children would place their shoes by the family hearth, hoping that St. Nicholas would leave treats in them. The Dutch called the saint "Sinter Klaas." When Dutch colonists settled in America, they continued this tradition. "Sinter Klaas" became known as Santa Claus.

1. **What legend started the Dutch tradition of placing shoes by the family hearth?**
   - Ⓐ Nicholas living in the fourth century
   - Ⓑ Nicholas throwing a bag of coins down a chimney
   - Ⓒ Nicholas being named a saint
   - Ⓓ the Dutch settling in America

2. **Which one of these is an opinion?**
   - Ⓕ Life would be dull without Santa Claus.
   - Ⓖ Nicholas was named a saint.
   - Ⓗ The Dutch children placed their shoes on the hearth.
   - Ⓙ The name "Sinter Klaas" became Santa Claus.

3. **This passage would be considered —**
   - Ⓐ science fiction.
   - Ⓑ historical fiction.
   - Ⓒ nonfiction.
   - Ⓓ fantasy.

═══ READING: COMPREHENSION ═══

● **Lesson 12: Fiction**

Directions: Read the passage. Choose the answer for each question that follows the passage.

Example

Misha stood on the stage. His hands shook so hard that he could barely hold his violin. A hush fell over the audience. He shut his eyes tight and remembered what his music teacher had told him—"You can do it. Take a deep breath and pretend that you're standing in your living room." Misha lifted his violin to his chin and played his solo perfectly from beginning to end.

A. **From this passage, what do you know about Misha?**

Ⓐ He has been playing the violin for many years.

Ⓑ He likes to play his violin in front of an audience.

Ⓒ He gets nervous when he is performing in front of others.

Ⓓ He and his music teacher are friends.

 Clue Read the questions first. Think about them as you read the passage.

● **Practice**

Floating the River

"Aren't we there yet?" Shiloh asked. At last, she and her family were on their way to their annual tubing trip. Floating down Glenn River on an inner tube was one of Shiloh's favorite things. This year they would float five whole miles, all the way to Glenn Fork.

With each passing mile, Shiloh smiled more and more as she thought of the fun they would have. When they finally reached Glenn Fork and parked the car, she jumped out, all ready to go.

"Not so fast, Shiloh," said her mother. "Remember, we're just here to leave the car. We still have to drive up the river. After we float back here, we'll be able to drive the car upstream to the truck. Otherwise, we won't have any way to get home."

"Oh, yeah, false alarm," Shiloh said. She had forgotten the family's plan to leave one car at each end of the float.

The whole family piled into the truck and drove to Jenkins Landing. Shiloh's father helped her unload her backpack and shiny tube from the truck. They walked down to the river's bank and put their toes in the water. Shiloh gasped as she felt how cold the water was. She took a deep breath and pushed herself out into the river. As Shiloh followed her family downstream, she thought to herself, "This will be the best tubing trip ever!"

GO ON ▷

READING: COMPREHENSION

● Lesson 12: Fiction (cont.)

1. This story is mostly about —
- Ⓐ driving a truck.
- Ⓑ a family's adventure.
- Ⓒ a family's argument.
- Ⓓ a family's business.

2. The family will float between which two points?
- Ⓕ from Jenkins Landing to Glenn Fork
- Ⓖ from Glenn Fork to Glenn River
- Ⓗ from Glenn River to Jenkins Landing
- Ⓙ from Glenn Fork to Jenkins Landing

3. How do you think Shiloh's parents feel about the tubing trip?
- Ⓐ bored
- Ⓑ disappointed
- Ⓒ frustrated
- Ⓓ excited

4. Why is the family driving both a car and a truck?
- Ⓕ so they don't get the truck wet and muddy
- Ⓖ so they can show that they have a lot of money
- Ⓗ so they can all have a ride to the river
- Ⓙ so they can have transportation back to where they started

5. Which character do you learn the most about in this passage?
- Ⓐ Shiloh's mother
- Ⓑ Shiloh
- Ⓒ Shiloh's father
- Ⓓ Shiloh's sister

6. When Shiloh says, "false alarm," she means —
- Ⓕ she didn't tell the truth.
- Ⓖ that there is no danger.
- Ⓗ she made a mistake.
- Ⓙ there's been a warning.

--- **READING: COMPREHENSION** ---

● Lesson 13: Fiction

Directions: Read the passage. Choose the answer for each question that follows the passage.

Example

Skyler had never been as scared as he was the first time he tried to go inline skating. His legs felt like jelly. The skates kept slipping out from under him. He had thought it would be a snap to soar through the air in jumps and spins, but he found out that skating isn't as easy as it looks. Skyler wasn't going to give up. He practiced and practiced until he started to improve. Finally he was able to skate without falling down. Skyler knew if he kept practicing that some day he would be able to do some jumps and spins too.

A. By the end of the passage, Skyler's feelings have changed from —

(A) proud ⟶ ashamed

(B) frightened ⟶ determined

(C) impatience ⟶ acceptance

(D) sadness ⟶ happiness

 Clue If you don't know the answer to a question, skip it and come back to it later.

● Practice

Survivors

As far as Kiki was concerned, the island had always been her home, and she loved it. She had been just about a year old when the ship she and her family had been on was caught in a great storm. She didn't remember their home in England, where she had been born, or boarding the ship for Australia. Kiki certainly didn't remember how her family and a few dozen others had arrived on the island in lifeboats, or even how they had built houses and made new lives.

The Martin family and the others who had survived the shipwreck had worked hard to make the island livable. In the weeks following the wreck, chests of seeds, tools, and food washed up on the beach. These chests gave the survivors a chance to build a new life on the island. Now, ten years after the disaster, the island was a wonderful place to live. Everyone had a comfortable home and there was plenty of food.

Kiki and the other children explored the island every day. It was on one of these outings that they saw the great ships. The children had climbed to the top of the highest peak on the island to study the sea birds that nested on the cliffs below. When they reached the top of the peak, Kiki spotted the four ships sailing toward the island.

GO ON ➡

READING: COMPREHENSION

● **Lesson 13: Fiction (cont.)**

By the time Kiki and her friends climbed down the mountain, the ships had reached the island and the captain and crew were surprised to find other English settlers there. They had known about the shipwreck, of course, but they had no idea there were survivors. The ships were heading to Australia, and the survivors were welcomed to join the crew on board.

That, however, was the problem. Almost all the survivors didn't want to leave the island, especially the children like Kiki who had spent most of their lives there or the dozen who had been born there. For them, the island was their world, and they couldn't imagine leaving it.

1. **What is the main idea of this story?**
   - (A) how people lived after a shipwreck
   - (B) explorers discovering a deserted island
   - (C) children studying sea birds
   - (D) a family's journey to Australia

2. **What helped the survivors begin their new lives on the island?**
   - (F) having the children explore the island
   - (G) memories of England
   - (H) the captain and crew of the ships sailing to Australia
   - (J) supplies that washed up on the beach

3. **If the children could vote on whether to leave the island or to stay, which of these would probably happen?**
   - (A) Most would vote to leave.
   - (B) Most would vote to stay.
   - (C) Most would not vote.
   - (D) There would be a tie.

4. **Which of the following sentences expresses an opinion?**
   - (F) Kiki didn't remember their home in England.
   - (G) The children had climbed to the top of the highest peak.
   - (H) The island was a wonderful place to live.
   - (J) The captain and crew were surprised to find other English settlers there.

5. **What do you know about the island from reading this passage?**
   - (A) The island has a desert climate.
   - (B) There are cliffs on the island.
   - (C) There are palm trees on the island.
   - (D) Dangerous animals live on the island.

6. **How do you suppose Kiki will feel if her family decides to leave the island?**
   - (F) disappointed
   - (G) excited
   - (H) proud
   - (J) happy

STOP

READING: COMPREHENSION

● **Lesson 14: Fiction**

Directions: Read the passage. Choose the answer for each question that follows the passage.

Example

Leo wrote an article called "Lizards" for the school paper. He didn't expect anyone to get excited about it, but they did. His teacher was pleased that Leo had done such a good job. "This was the best story you ever wrote," she said. "I'm going to enter it in the state writing competition for you. Maybe you'll win a prize!"

A. How do you think Leo felt about his teacher's reaction to his article?

- Ⓐ afraid
- Ⓑ unhappy
- Ⓒ embarrassed
- Ⓓ surprised

Clue If you know which answer is correct, mark it and move on to the next questions.

● **Practice**

The Story of Arachne

Long ago in a far away country lived a young woman named Arachne. She was not rich or beautiful, but she had one great talent. Arachne could weave the most beautiful cloth anyone had ever seen. Everyone in Arachne's village talked about her wonderful cloth, and soon she became famous. But as her fame grew, so did her pride.

"No one else can weave as well as I can," Arachne boasted. "Not even the goddess Minerva could make anything so lovely and fine."

Now Minerva wove cloth for all the gods. She was proud of her weaving too and thought that no human could ever match her skills. Soon Arachne's words reached Minerva's ears and the goddess became angry.

"So the human woman thinks she is better than I!" Minerva roared. "We will see about that!"

Minerva searched the countryside until she came upon Arachne's home. Minerva called to Arachne and challenged her to a contest. "Let us both weave a length of cloth. We will see whose is the most beautiful."

READING: COMPREHENSION

● **Lesson 14: Fiction (cont.)**

Arachne agreed. She set up two looms, and she and Minerva went to work. The goddess wove cloth of all the colors of the rainbow. It sparkled in the sun and floated on the breeze like a butterfly. But Arachne wove cloth that sparkled like gold and jewels. The villagers were dazzled by Arachne's cloth. When Minerva inspected it, she knew Arachne was the best weaver.

Minerva was enraged. She took out a jar of magic water and sprinkled it on Arachne. Instantly, poor Arachne began to change. She shrank smaller and smaller until she could almost not be seen. She grew more arms and became covered in fine brown hair. When it was all over, Arachne had become a tiny brown spider. Arachne would never boast again, but she would spend the rest of her life weaving fine webs.

1. People in ancient times made up stories, or myths, to explain things in their world that they did not understand. This myth explains —
   - (A) how to weave cloth.
   - (B) why spiders weave webs.
   - (C) how to turn a person into a spider.
   - (D) why it is wrong to be boastful.

Here is a sequence of events that happens in the passage.

Arachne becomes a famous weaver.
Arachne brags that her skills are better than the goddess Minerva's.
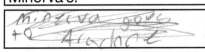
Minerva realizes that Arachne is the better weaver.

2. Which of these events should go in the empty box?
   - (F) Minerva sprinkles water on Arachne.
   - (G) Minerva changes Arachne into a spider.
   - (H) Minerva challenges Arachne to a weaving contest.
   - (J) Arachne weaves webs.

3. What might have happened if Arachne had not bragged about her talents?
   - (A) Minerva would have left her alone.
   - (B) Arachne would not have become famous.
   - (C) The villagers would not have appreciated Arachne's weaving.
   - (D) Minerva would not be allowed to make cloth for the gods anymore.

4. What caused Minerva to challenge Arachne to the contest?
   - (F) boredom and skill
   - (G) contentment and humility
   - (H) fear and confusion
   - (J) pride and jealousy

5. This passage tells us the most about the —
   - (A) plot.
   - (B) mood.
   - (C) characters.
   - (D) setting.

6. This story might have been told to remind people not to —
   - (F) brag about their talents.
   - (G) weave cloth.
   - (H) enter competitions.
   - (J) kill spiders.

═══════════════ READING: COMPREHENSION ═══════════════

● **Lesson 15: Reading Literature**

Directions: Read the poem. Choose the best answers to the questions that follow.

Black-Eyed Rebel
by Will Carleton

A boy drove into the city, his wagon loaded down

With food to feed the people of the British-governed town;

And the little black-eyed rebel, so innocent and sly,

Was watching for his coming from the corner of her eye.

…He drove up to the market, he waited in the line;

His apples and potatoes were fresh and fair and fine;

But long and long he waited, and no one came to buy,

Save the black-eyed rebel, watching from the corner of her eye.

…For she knew that 'neath the lining of the coat he wore that day,

Were long letters from the husbands and the fathers far away,

Who were fighting for the freedom that they meant to gain or die;

And a tear like silver glistened in the corner of her eye.

But the treasures—how to get them? crept the questions though her mind,

Since keen enemies were watching for what prizes they might find;

And she paused a while and pondered, with a pretty little sigh;

Then resolve crept through her features, and shrewdness fired her eye.

So she resolutely walked up to the wagon old and red;

"May I have a dozen apples for a kiss?" she sweetly said;

And the brown face flushed to scarlet; for the boy was somewhat shy,

And he saw her laughing at him from the corner of her eye.

...Clinging round his brawny neck, she clasped her fingers white and small,

And then whispered, "Quick! the letters! thrust them underneath my shawl!"

Carry back again this package, and be sure that you are spry!"

And she sweetly smiled upon him from the corner of her eye.

...With the news of loved ones absent to the dear friends they would greet,

Searching them who hungered for them, swift she glided through the street.

"There is nothing worth the doing that it does not pay to try,"

Thought the little black-eyed rebel, with a twinkle in her eye.

READING: COMPREHENSION

● Lesson 15: Reading Literature (cont.)

1. **What word best describes the interaction between the boy and the black-eyed rebel?**
   - (A) peaceful
   - (B) dangerous
   - (C) prosperous
   - (D) happy

2. **How does the author tell the story?**
   - (F) in the order in which it happened
   - (G) in a different order than how it happened
   - (H) by only telling facts
   - (J) by only telling feelings

3. **How are the boy and the girl alike?**
   - (A) They are hungry.
   - (B) They are British.
   - (C) They are selling fruits and vegetables.
   - (D) They are rebels.

4. **What happens first in the poem?**
   - (F) The girl kisses the boy.
   - (G) The boy gives the girl letters.
   - (H) The boy tries to sell fruit and vegetables.
   - (J) The boy brings a wagon of fruit and vegetables to town.

5. **What is the theme of the poem?**
   - (A) It is good to be sneaky.
   - (B) Sometimes, you have to try something unusual to get what you want.
   - (C) Desperate times require desperate action.
   - (D) It's always right to fight against an enemy.

6. **What line from the poem best summarizes the text?**
   - (F) Then resolve crept through her features, and shrewdness fired her eye.
   - (G) "May I have a dozen apples for a kiss?" she sweetly said;
   - (H) "There is nothing worth the doing that it does not pay to try,"
   - (J) Searching them who hungered for them, swift she glided through the street.

7. **In the third stanza, *a tear like silver glistened* in the girl's eye. This line contains an example of which type of figurative language?**
   - (A) metaphor
   - (B) personification
   - (C) foreshadowing
   - (D) simile

8. **The boy and girl are _____ because they break the law to get news to the people.**
   - (F) soldiers
   - (G) loyal
   - (H) rebels
   - (J) cowards

READING: COMPREHENSION

● Lesson 16: Parts of a Story

Directions: Read each item. Fill in the circle next to the answer you think is correct.

Example

It was Saturday morning. All the world was smiling and bright—all, that is, except Tom Sawyer. With his pail of whitewash and a large brush, Tom stared sadly at the long fence. He dipped his brush into the white glop and began the job of whitewashing the fence.

A. This passage tells us about a boy named Tom Sawyer. How does Tom feel about whitewashing the fence?

- (A) glum
- (B) joyful
- (C) excited
- (D) cheerful

 Clue Skim the passage then read the questions. Go back to the passage to find the answers to the questions.

● Practice

One day, just as the leaves were beginning to change color, Rip Van Winkle walked through the woods and up the mountains. By early afternoon he found himself on one of the highest points of the Catskill Mountains. By late afternoon Rip was tired and panting, so he found a spot with a beautiful view where he could lay down and rest. Through an opening in the trees, Rip could see miles and miles of lower country and rich woodland. In the distance he could view the mighty Hudson River. It was moving calmly along its course, showing reflections of the soft white clouds in the sky.

1. **What part of a story does this passage tell about?**
   - (A) the setting
   - (B) the plot
   - (C) the conflict
   - (D) the characters

2. **How do you think Rip feels about where he is?**
   - (F) He thinks it is exciting.
   - (G) He thinks it is annoying.
   - (H) He thinks it is peaceful.
   - (J) He thinks it is dangerous.

3. **Where in a story would you most likely find this passage?**
   - (A) near the beginning
   - (B) in the middle
   - (C) near the end
   - (D) in the table of contents

4. **At what time of year does this passage take place?**
   - (F) winter
   - (G) spring
   - (H) summer
   - (J) fall

 STOP

═══ READING: COMPREHENSION ═══

● Lesson 17: Nonfiction

Directions: Read the passage. Choose the answer for each question that follows the passage.

Example

Wasps build new nests every year. The potter wasp creates a mud "jar" nest for each of its eggs. The wasp then stings caterpillars to paralyze them and places them in the jar nests. The nests are sealed and the caterpillars are used as food for the developing wasps.

A. How does the potter wasp paralyze caterpillars?
- (A) by stinging them
- (B) by spitting on them
- (C) by biting them
- (D) by sealing them in jars

 Clue Look for important facts in the passage. These facts may be used in the questions that follow.

● Practice

Exploring a Coral Reef

A coral reef is a beautiful undersea wilderness filled with fascinating plants and animals. It is one of the most populated environments on Earth. Coral reefs are found where ocean water is warm, clean, and shallow.

For hundreds of years, people thought that coral was a type of flowering plant. Amazingly, coral reefs are actually formed by little tube-shaped animals called coral polyps. Coral polyps have hard outer skeletons that cover and protect their soft bodies. Most coral polyps stay within their protective skeletons during the day. At night, fingerlike tentacles emerge from the skeleton and pull tiny animals into the coral's mouth. When the coral polyps die, their skeletons remain in place. New polyps make their homes on the rocky foundations of the skeletons. In this way, the reef grows larger and larger.

Living things take up every bit of space on a coral reef. Beautiful tropical fish swim among sea turtles, colorful marine worms, and giant clams. Sharks patrol the water looking for food. Sea cucumbers share the rocky, sandy bottom of the reef with sea urchins. At dusk, octopuses come out of their caves and begin searching for food.

Many people come to coral reefs to snorkel or scuba dive. They swim in the water and explore the beauty of the reef. Unfortunately, some people damage the reefs by handling the coral. It may take hundreds of years for a reef to restore itself after a careless person damages it.

 GO ON

READING: COMPREHENSION

● **Lesson 17: Nonfiction (cont.)**

1. **What is the main idea of this passage?**
    - (A) Coral polyps are animals, not plants.
    - (B) People should handle coral.
    - (C) A coral reef is a delicate habitat populated by a wide array of animals.
    - (D) Coral reefs need warm, clean, and shallow ocean water to survive.

2. **How do coral polyps eat?**
    - (F) Tentacles emerge and capture tiny animals.
    - (G) Tropical fish bring them food.
    - (H) Tiny animals cling to the skeletons.
    - (J) They are hand-fed by people.

3. **How does the author of this passage feel about coral reefs?**
    - (A) The author would not want to visit a coral reef.
    - (B) The author thinks reefs are easily replaced.
    - (C) The author thinks reefs are hideous.
    - (D) The author thinks reefs are beautiful.

4. **Which of these sentences expresses an opinion?**
    - (F) Coral polyps have hard outer skeletons that cover and protect their soft bodies.
    - (G) Some people damage the reefs by handling the coral.
    - (H) A coral reef is a beautiful undersea wilderness.
    - (J) Coral reefs are found where ocean water is warm, clean, and shallow.

5. **Where would a passage like this be most likely to appear?**
    - (A) in a nature magazine
    - (B) in an almanac
    - (C) in a thesaurus
    - (D) in a biography

6. **Which of these is not explained in the passage?**
    - (F) how coral polyps eat
    - (G) that people used to think coral was a plant
    - (H) how pollution damages reefs
    - (J) other types of animals that live in and around reefs

READING: COMPREHENSION

● Lesson 18: Nonfiction

Directions: Read the passage. Choose the answer for each question that follows the passage.

Example

Laura Ingalls Wilder wrote a series of nine children's books about her life as a pioneer. The first book was titled *Little House in the Big Woods*. Laura's books have been praised for their portrayals of life on the American frontier.

A.   What would be a good title for this passage?

- Ⓐ Little Laura
- Ⓑ The American Frontier
- Ⓒ Writing Children's Books
- Ⓓ Laura Ingalls Wilder: Pioneer and Author

 Clue **Skim the passage, then read the questions. Refer back to the passage to find the answers. You don't have to read the story over again for each question.**

● Practice

Swimming Star

Every day, thousands of people cross the channel of water between France and England in planes, ferries, and even trains. An American athlete, Gertrude Caroline Ederle, however, used a different method. She was the first woman to swim across the English Channel.

Gertrude Ederle was born in New York City in 1906. She dedicated herself to the sport of swimming at an early age and enjoyed great success. Before long, she was on her way to becoming one of the most famous American swimmers of her time. When she was sixteen, Ederle broke seven records in one day at a swimming competition in New York. Two years later, in 1924, she represented the United States at the Olympic Games, winning a gold medal in the 400-meter freestyle relay.

After her Olympic victory, she looked for an even greater challenge. One of the most difficult swims is to cross the 21-mile wide English Channel. The seas in the channel can be rough, and the water is cold. In the past, the feat had only been accomplished by male swimmers. Most people believed that the swim was too difficult for a woman, but Ederle wanted to prove them wrong. She didn't make it on her first attempt, but in 1926 she tried again. Leaving from the coast of France, Ederle had to swim even longer than planned because of heavy seas. She went an extra fourteen miles and still managed to beat the world record by almost two hours. This accomplishment made her an instant heroine at the age of twenty.

READING: COMPREHENSION

● Lesson 18: Nonfiction (cont.)

1. **What is the main idea of the passage?**
    - (A) Swimming is a fun sport.
    - (B) Winning an Olympic medal will make you wealthy.
    - (C) If you want to be very successful at something, you have to start at a young age.
    - (D) Hard work and dedication can lead to great success.

2. **Which event happened first in the passage about Ederle's life?**
    - (F) She swam across the English Channel.
    - (G) She broke seven swimming records in a single day of competition.
    - (H) She won an Olympic gold medal.
    - (J) She looked for more challenges.

3. **Based on the information in the passage, what word probably describes Ederle's personality?**
    - (A) imaginative
    - (B) passive
    - (C) lazy
    - (D) determined

4. **Why did Ederle decide to swim across the English Channel?**
    - (F) someone dared her to
    - (G) to earn a lot of money
    - (H) to prove that women could to do it
    - (J) to win a gold medal

5. **Which sentence would describe what the water was like on the day Ederle swam across the channel?**
    - (A) The water was cold and choppy.
    - (B) The water was calm and warm.
    - (C) The water was shallow.
    - (D) The water was frozen.

6. **According to the passage, why was Ederle considered a heroine?**
    - (F) because she was a generous person
    - (G) because she had done something that no other woman had ever done
    - (H) because she was a great swimmer
    - (J) because she rescued someone

READING: COMPREHENSION

● **Lesson 19: Nonfiction**

Directions: Read the passage. Choose the answer for each question that follows the passage.

Example

Ice hockey originated in the mid-1800s, when British troops played games of field hockey on the frozen lakes and ponds of Canada's provinces of Ontario and Nova Scotia. It became Canada's national sport by the early 1900s. Since then, the sport has become popular in European countries such as Russia and Sweden, as well as in the United States.

A. **Where would a passage like this be most likely to appear?**

  (A) in an atlas

  (B) in a medical journal

  (C) in a dictionary

  (D) in a book on the history of sports

Once you have chosen an answer, move on to the next question. Only change an answer if you are certain that it is wrong.

● **Practice**

Jackie Robinson

Jackie Robinson, born in 1919, was the first African-American man to play modern American major league baseball. In high school and college, he played many sports. He earned letters in track and field, basketball, football, and baseball. Unfortunately, Robinson had to quit college for financial reasons. It seemed his days of playing sports were over.

In 1942, Robinson was drafted into the army. He faced a lot of prejudice in the army. As an officer, he was asked to join the army football team. But when other teams objected to playing against a team with a black member, he turned to the army baseball team. There, he was rejected again because of his race.

After leaving the army in 1945, Robinson played shortstop for the Kansas City Monarchs, one of several teams in the Negro League. Professional baseball was still segregated at that time, but the Brooklyn Dodgers' president, Branch Rickey, recognized Robinson's athletic skills. Rickey was determined to make Robinson the first African-American player in major league baseball.

GO ON

READING: COMPREHENSION

● Lesson 19: Nonfiction (cont.)

Robinson started playing with the Dodgers' farm team. Rickey advised Robinson not to fight back when people were unkind to him. Baseball players and fans alike thought he should not be allowed to play. But he played so well that in 1947, he joined the Brooklyn Dodgers.

At first his teammates didn't like playing with him; however, when other people screamed at him, they came to his defense. Because of his great performance at second base and his outstanding batting average, Robinson was selected Rookie of the Year. In 1949, he was named the Most Valuable Player in the National League. One of his greatest thrills was when he helped the Dodgers win the 1955 World Series.

Jackie Robinson paved the way for African-American men to play in the major leagues. In 1962, he was inducted into baseball's Hall of Fame. Ten years later, at the age of 53, Robinson died in Stamford, Connecticut.

1. **What would be a good title for the passage?**
   - (A) Jackie Robinson: A Major League Success
   - (B) Rickey and Robinson Make it to the Majors
   - (C) How to Play Second Base
   - (D) The Baseball Hall of Fame

2. **Why was Robinson selected as Rookie of the Year?**
   - (F) for his batting average and his skills at second base
   - (G) for his excellent attitude
   - (H) for his skills as a shortstop
   - (J) because he helped win the World Series

3. **How do you think Jackie Robinson felt toward Branch Rickey?**
   - (A) hostile
   - (B) disgusted
   - (C) appreciative
   - (D) embarrassed

4. **What effect did segregation have on professional baseball?**
   - (F) White players were given the best positions.
   - (G) Anyone with enough talent was invited to play.
   - (H) People who did not graduate from college could not play professional baseball.
   - (J) African Americans weren't allowed to play in the major leagues.

5. **How do you think Robinson felt about his accomplishments?**
   - (A) disappointed
   - (B) proud
   - (C) dissatisfied
   - (D) shy

6. **Why did Robinson join the army?**
   - (F) He needed a job.
   - (G) He wanted to travel.
   - (H) He was drafted.
   - (J) He didn't know what else to do after he left college.

═══════════════ **READING: COMPREHENSION** ═══════════════

● **Lesson 20: Reading Informational Text**

Directions: Read the texts. Choose the best answers to the questions that follow.

Wolf Ways

Wolves are often pictured in fairy tales as ferocious animals, always ready to attack and kill. The three little pigs flee from the "big, bad wolf." Little Red Riding Hood must beware of the wolf that dresses up like Grandma and wants to eat her. But are wolves really that vicious?

Wolves are social animals that live together in packs of two to 20 individuals. Each pack has a male and a female leader called the *alpha wolves.* The leaders are usually the strongest and healthiest. Typically, only the alpha female has cubs. The members of a pack generally cooperate and get along with one another.

Wolves are often pictured howling at the moon. Scientists have discovered that the howl is actually a way of locating other wolves, assembling the pack, sounding an alarm, or announcing a kill. Besides their howl, wolves use body language to communicate. The positions of their backs, necks, ears, and tails send distinct messages that other wolves understand. A wolf with its ears and tail up is high-ranking. A wolf with its tail down is showing submission.

Wolves feed on large animals such as deer and elk, with the pack working together to bring down prey. They kill only when they are hungry and need to eat.

Who are the worst enemies of wolves? Humans! Wolves are more likely to run from people than to attack, but because of their ferocious reputation, they have been hunted and killed for years. Wolves were once common across much of North America, but they are now rare and can be found only in remote wooded regions.

One Opinion

I live in Montana near Yellowstone National Park. During the 1990s, 41 wild wolves were released in the park. Scientists hoped their population would grow so that wolves would no longer be an endangered species. That plan has succeeded. Today, more than 1,600 wolves live in Idaho, Montana, and Wyoming.

I admire the wild beauty of wolves. However, knowing that they live near my home, I am afraid. On rare occasions, wolves attack humans. I want to protect my two young children when they play outside. I do not support wolf restoration efforts.

READING: COMPREHENSION

● Lesson 20: Reading Informational Text (cont.)

1. **How do pack members interact with each other?**
   - (A) They get along and work together.
   - (B) They fight among themselves.
   - (C) They ignore each other.
   - (D) They separate into smaller groups.

2. **Which text gives an opinion and reasons to support it?**
   - (F) *Wolf Ways*
   - (G) *One Opinion*
   - (H) both texts
   - (J) neither text

3. **What is the relationship between the alpha wolves and other wolves in the pack?**
   - (A) All the wolves are equals.
   - (B) The alpha wolves are the lowest members of the pack.
   - (C) The alpha wolves are the leaders of the pack.
   - (D) The alpha wolves do all the hunting for the rest of the pack.

4. **What is the structure of *Wolf Ways*?**
   - (F) It tells the story of wolves in chronological order.
   - (G) It compares wolves to other animals.
   - (H) It provides reasons to dispute fears about wolves.
   - (J) It shows the effect wolves have on the environment.

5. **Which statement about the two authors' points of view is true?**
   - (A) They are both afraid of wolves.
   - (B) They both like seeing wolves.
   - (C) The second author is more afraid of wolves than the first author.
   - (D) The first author is more afraid of wolves than the second author.

6. **What would be the best place to find the current number of wolves in Yellowstone Park?**
   - (F) an article with tips on visiting the park
   - (G) an encyclopedia article about the park
   - (H) an updated National Park Service Web site
   - (J) the glossary of a book about wolves

7. **After reading both texts, what do you know about wolves?**
   - (A) They are dangerous animals that are a threat to people.
   - (B) They are fascinating animals, but people are still afraid of them.
   - (C) The wolf population in Yellowstone Park is increasing.
   - (D) The wolf population is in danger from humans.

8. **What does *remote* mean?**
   - (F) lonely
   - (G) close by
   - (H) dangerous
   - (J) far away

READING: COMPREHENSION
SAMPLE TEST

Directions: Read the passage. Choose the answer for each question that follows the passage.

Example

Cats were first kept as pets in 2500 B.C. by the Egyptians. These first house cats were probably a type of wildcat called a Caffre cat. The idea of keeping a cat as a pet spread to Europe. Caffre cats were brought to Europe and are the ancestors of many of the modern cat breeds.

A. Europeans probably thought that keeping cats as pets was—

- (A) ridiculous.
- (B) a health hazard.
- (C) a good idea.
- (D) dangerous.

Here is a story about two seabirds. Read the story and then answer questions 1 through 4.

The penguin is a seabird that is native to the waters of the Southern Hemisphere. Penguins cannot fly, but they are excellent swimmers. They spend most of their time out at sea but come to land to raise their young. Mother penguins lay one or two eggs each season.

Puffins are another kind of seabird, but they are native to the cold waters of the Northern Hemisphere. Puffins can fly, but not very well. Like penguins, they swim well and spend most of their time out at sea. Mother puffins lay only one egg each season and they raise their young on land.

1. This story mostly describes —
- (A) how seabirds raise their young.
- (B) how penguins and puffins are alike and different.
- (C) how penguins and puffins swim.
- (D) where penguins and puffins live.

2. Which of the following statements is true?
- (F) Penguins live in the Northern Hemisphere.
- (G) Puffins live in the Northern Hemisphere.
- (H) Puffins lay more eggs than penguins.
- (J) Both birds spend most of their time on land.

3. Given what you know from reading the passage, what do you think penguins most likely eat?
- (A) fish
- (B) other birds
- (C) puffins
- (D) eggs

4. Which of these is a true statement about how penguins and puffins are alike?
- (F) The birds live in the Southern Hemisphere.
- (G) The birds lay 17 eggs each season.
- (H) The birds can fly for long distances.
- (J) The birds are good swimmers.

GO ON

Name _____ Date_____

Here is a story about the first battle of the Civil War. Read the story and then answer questions 5 through 10 on page 41.

The Flying Congressman

The first major battle of the Civil War was fought near the small town of Manassas Junction, Virginia. The Union army called the battle Bull Run, after the creek by that name. Inasmuch as this quaint little town lay just 30 miles southwest of Washington, D.C., a number of citizens from the nation's capital thought it might be fun to pack a picnic lunch, load up the family, and take a buggy ride out to watch the Confederates "get what was coming to them." They viewed the upcoming battle as nothing more than a sporting event. Even members of Congress were in attendance. No fewer than six senators and an undetermined number of congressmen showed up, as did pretty ladies in fancy gowns, all traveling in style in expensive buggies and carriages.

One particular congressman provided what turned out to be the only entertainment of the day for the spectators from the big city. What was predicted to be an easy victory for the Union forces turned into a rout. Federal troops retreated to the capital at a record pace, followed by carriages of Washington's elite—minus their picnic baskets. These were discarded when the rout began, and the Confederate soldiers had a feast when the battle was over.

Although those in flight were preoccupied with their safety, they could not help noticing a tall, long-legged congressman who, on foot, was leading the pack in its frantic race back to the capital. He was seen jumping ditches and gullies, and was said to have cleared a six-foot fence with a foot to spare. Many of the terror-stricken refugees howled with laughter, despite their fear.

History does not relate the name of the fleet and agile congressman. But there is a chance he might be the same legislator who, after reaching the safety of the capital, was confronted by President Lincoln. The President glared at the panting legislator and is supposed to have said dryly, "I congratulate you on winning the race!"

GO ON

5. **This story mostly shows that —**
   - (A) many people died at the Battle of Bull Run.
   - (B) congressmen during the Civil War were quite athletic.
   - (C) some people in Washington, D.C., did not take the beginning of the Civil War seriously.
   - (D) the Confederates would win the war.

6. **According to the story, who ended up eating the picnic lunches?**
   - (F) the Washington elite
   - (G) President Lincoln
   - (H) the Union soldiers
   - (J) the Confederate soldiers

7. **Reread the last sentence of the story. How do you suppose the President felt about the people who went to watch the battle?**
   - (A) He was angry with them.
   - (B) He was worried about them.
   - (C) He was proud of them.
   - (D) He distrusted them.

8. **Why did the spectators run away from the battle?**
   - (F) because the Union soldiers were winning the battle
   - (G) because they had lost their picnic baskets
   - (H) because they were in buggies
   - (J) because the Union soldiers were losing the battle

9. **This story tells us the most about —**
   - (A) Manassas Junction, Virginia.
   - (B) why the Civil War took place.
   - (C) the people who went to watch the battle.
   - (D) President Lincoln's approach to the war.

10. **Why was the battle named "Bull Run"?**
    - (F) because that was the name of the nearest town
    - (G) because the people had to run away
    - (H) because that was the name of a nearby creek
    - (J) because the Confederates liked the name

GO ON

Name _____ Date_____

READING: COMPREHENSION
SAMPLE TEST (cont.)

Here is a story about a day at a baseball game. Read the story and answer questions 11 through 16 on page 43.

Bonkers for Baseball

I remember a special Mother's Day back in 1939. My mom was a big baseball fan so my father treated us to tickets for the Brainford Bisons game. We sat in box seats owned by my father's company. It was an exciting day.

Before the game began, we started talking to a woman sitting in a nearby box seat. We learned that she was the mother of the Beulah Blaze's pitcher. Her son, Brian Falls, had been pitching in the minor leagues for three years. This was the first time she had ever seen him pitch in a professional game.

For the special event, Brian Falls had treated his mother to a box seat. He had the box decorated in flowers. Mrs. Falls was so excited. She told us that she had always encouraged Brian to become a baseball player. Her dream for her son had come true.

My team wasn't doing very well in the early innings. With Brian Falls pitching, the Brainford Bisons' batters kept striking out. Then, Falls threw a fastball to the plate. The batter swung at it. He caught a piece of it and fouled it off. The foul ball flew into the crowd. It came straight toward us! My dad and I reached into the air to catch it, but the ball veered left and hit Mrs. Falls in the head. She was knocked unconscious. We couldn't believe it—out of all the people in the stands, the ball hit the pitcher's mother! Mrs. Falls was rushed to the hospital. For the rest of the game we wondered what had happened to her. Later we learned the rest of the story.

Brian Falls left the game to accompany his mom to the hospital. He was so upset that he told her he would quit the game. His mother, who was recovering nicely, convinced him to stay in baseball. It's a good thing, because 3 years later he joined the major leagues.

READING: COMPREHENSION
SAMPLE TEST (cont.)

11. What would be another good title for this story?

- (A) Mother's Day at the Ballpark
- (B) Making It in the Majors
- (C) Brian Falls: His Career in Baseball
- (D) The Brainsford Bisons Steal Home

Here is a time line of what happens in the story.

| The family goes to the baseball game for Mother's Day. |

| |

| A foul ball is hit into the stands. |

| Brian Falls joins the major leagues. |

12. Which of these events should go in the empty box?

- (F) Mrs. Falls convinces Brian not to quit baseball.
- (G) Mrs. Falls is taken to the hospital.
- (H) The family discovers that the woman they've been talking with is the mother of the Beulah Blaze's pitcher.
- (J) The ball is almost caught by the narrator.

13. Why do you suppose Brian Falls had his mother's box seat decorated with flowers?

- (A) because he wanted to impress his friends
- (B) because it was the first time she had seen him pitch professionally
- (C) because he was in the major leagues
- (D) because she told him not to quit

14. Why was Mrs. Falls taken to the hospital?

- (F) because she needed to tell Brian to stay in the game
- (G) because she was a nurse
- (H) because she was sick
- (J) because she was hit by a foul ball

15. Mrs. Falls probably taught Brian to —

- (A) follow his dreams.
- (B) give up when things got too hard.
- (C) play baseball.
- (D) fight against his opponents.

16. From reading the passage, how do you suppose the narrator feels about baseball?

- (F) He thinks it's a silly game.
- (G) He despises it.
- (H) He is bored with it.
- (J) He enjoys it.

GO ON

READING: COMPREHENSION
SAMPLE TEST (cont.)

Read this story about a special dinner. Then answer questions 17 through 22 on page 45.

A Delicious Dinner

Molly's family is Chinese-American. They serve a traditional Chinese meal once a week. Molly invited her friend Amy to join them this week.

Molly's family was busy preparing for dinner when Amy arrived. The house was filled with many good smells. "You can help me set the table," Molly told her friend. They laid the place settings on the table. They gave each person a pair of chopsticks, a soup bowl, a soup spoon, and a rice bowl on a saucer.

"Where are the forks and knives?" Amy asked

"Oh, you won't need those," Molly explained. "We use chopsticks. But don't worry. I'll show you how to use them."

The two girls went into the kitchen. Molly's father was slicing and chopping vegetables. He threw the vegetables into a large cooking pan coated with hot oil.

"That's a wok," Molly said.

Amy watched the vegetables sizzle. Then Molly's mother asked the girls to carry platters of food to the table. Amy carried the steamed rice. It was one of the few dishes she recognized. There were meat-filled bundles called won-tons, steamed noodles, stir-fried beef, sweet-and-sour chicken, and pork spareribs. The food was nutritious and seasoned with herbs, spices, and sauces.

Amy was a little nervous about eating with chopsticks. Molly gave her instructions on how to hold and pinch with the chopsticks.

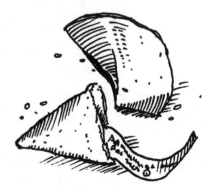

Amy managed to pick up a piece of chicken in her chopsticks. Suddenly, her fingers slipped and the chicken flew across the table. It landed in Molly's soup with a splash. Everyone smiled. "We keep these on hand for emergencies," Molly's father said kindly. He brought out a knife and fork and handed them to Amy. Amy was relieved and ate her dinner. It was delicious!

At the end of the meal, Amy was given a fortune cookie. She broke it open and read the fortune inside. It said, "If you practice hard, you will learn many things." Amy laughed and said, "If you let me take home a pair of chopsticks, my fortune may come true!"

GO ON

READING: COMPREHENSION
SAMPLE TEST (cont.)

17. This story is mostly about —
    - (A) Chinese food.
    - (B) a family's traditions.
    - (C) a girl trying to use chopsticks.
    - (D) what it takes to have friends.

18. What food was the most familiar to Amy?
    - (F) sweet-and-sour chicken
    - (G) rice
    - (H) won-tons
    - (J) steamed noodles

19. How do you think Molly's parents felt when Amy dropped her food?
    - (A) They understood that Amy wasn't used to using chopsticks.
    - (B) They felt Amy had insulted their culture.
    - (C) They thought Amy had bad manners.
    - (D) They wished Amy hadn't come to dinner.

20. Why did Amy's fortune make her laugh?
    - (F) because she was trying to act brave
    - (G) because she spilled her food
    - (H) because she thought it was a joke
    - (J) because she knew she needed to practice using chopsticks

21. In this story, we learn the most about —
    - (A) Molly
    - (B) Amy
    - (C) Molly's mother
    - (D) Molly's father

22. Molly's father said, "We keep these on hand for emergencies." What was he referring to?
    - (F) platters of food
    - (G) a wok
    - (H) a knife and fork
    - (J) chopsticks

STOP

READING PRACTICE TEST

● Part 1: Vocabulary

Directions: Read each item. Fill in the circle next to the correct answer.

Examples

Choose the word that means the same or about the same as the underlined word.

A.   filled with grief

- Ⓐ sorrow
- Ⓑ cheer
- Ⓒ admiration
- Ⓓ worry

Choose the word that means the opposite of the underlined word.

B.   determined attitude

- Ⓕ difficult
- Ⓖ wavering
- Ⓗ courageous
- Ⓙ enduring

For numbers 1–4, choose the word that means the same or about the same as the underlined word.

1.   a bundle of goods

- Ⓐ sweater
- Ⓑ burden
- Ⓒ rumble
- Ⓓ package

2.   restore the wood

- Ⓕ repair
- Ⓖ retread
- Ⓗ relieve
- Ⓙ reduce

3.   The dishes clattered in the sink. Clattered means —

- Ⓐ rattled
- Ⓑ broke
- Ⓒ jumped
- Ⓓ washed

4.   Max planted a sapling in the yard. A sapling is a —

- Ⓕ type of vegetable
- Ⓖ flower
- Ⓗ shrub
- Ⓙ young tree

For numbers 5–8, choose the word that means the opposite of the underlined word.

5.   scamper away

- Ⓐ run
- Ⓑ jog
- Ⓒ stroll
- Ⓓ sprint

6.   contemporary art

- Ⓕ modern
- Ⓖ ancient
- Ⓗ imaginative
- Ⓙ folksy

7.   the collapse of the government

- Ⓐ creation
- Ⓑ structure
- Ⓒ downfall
- Ⓓ laws

8.   reckless behavior

- Ⓕ foolish
- Ⓖ carefree
- Ⓗ juvenile
- Ⓙ thoughtful

GO ON

Name _____ Date _____

For numbers 9 and 10, choose the word that best completes both sentences.

9. Jennifer plays in a _____.
   Use a rubber _____ to keep the papers together.
   - (A) group
   - (B) ribbon
   - (C) band
   - (D) string

10. What is the _____ of your birth?
    His family has a _____ farm.
    - (F) date
    - (G) month
    - (H) citrus
    - (J) year

For number 11, read the item. Fill in the circle next to the correct answer.

11. The ship sailed into the **bay**.

    In which sentence does the word **bay** mean the same thing as in the sentence above?
    - (A) The bay horse was my favorite.
    - (B) Coyotes bay at the moon.
    - (C) Johan sat in the bay window.
    - (D) Marnie found buried treasure at the bottom of the bay.

For numbers 12 and 13, choose the answer that best defines the underlined part.

12. <u>tri</u>athlon   <u>tri</u>angle
    - (F) two
    - (G) three
    - (H) four
    - (J) five

13. teach<u>er</u>   wait<u>er</u>
    - (A) the study of
    - (B) small
    - (C) art or skill of
    - (D) one who

14. Which of these words probably comes from the Latin word *bini oculus* meaning "two eyes at a time"?
    - (F) bindery
    - (G) bingo
    - (H) binoculars
    - (J) binomial

15. Which of these words probably comes from the Italian word *ombra* meaning "shade"?
    - (A) umbrella
    - (B) omelette
    - (C) omit
    - (D) umpire

READING PRACTICE TEST
Part 1: Vocabulary (cont.)

Read the paragraph. Choose the word that best fits in each numbered blank.

The armadillo is ____(16)____ in several ways. First, the female gives birth to four babies, and they are always the same sex. Second, when an armadillo is ____(17)____ and cannot escape to its ____(18)____ or quickly dig itself into the ground, it rolls itself into a tight, protective ball. This is possible because of the joined, ____(19)____ plates of its shell. The armadillo also tucks in its head and feet. If, by chance, it ____(20)____ to reach the safety of its burrow, the armadillo can hold on so tightly with its strong claws that it is virtually ____(21)____ to pull it out.

16.
- (F) honored
- (G) unusual
- (H) motivated
- (J) typical

17.
- (A) assisted
- (B) free
- (C) cornered
- (D) released

18.
- (F) burrow
- (G) vehicle
- (H) porch
- (J) dormitory

19.
- (A) overlapping
- (B) detached
- (C) soft
- (D) disconnected

20.
- (F) endeavors
- (G) insists
- (H) actually
- (J) manages

21.
- (A) simple
- (B) impossible
- (C) likely
- (D) difficult

STOP

READING PRACTICE TEST

● Part 2: Comprehension

Directions: Read the passage. Choose the answer for each question that follows the passage.

Example

When hunting, meerkats take turns at guard duty. Standing ramrod straight on its hind legs, the meerkat on duty scans the sky and horizon for predators. If an enemy is spotted, the alert sentry sounds a shrill alarm, and its fellow meerkats run for cover.

A. **Why do meerkats take turns keeping guard?**

(A) to prove that they can cooperate

(B) to allow the mother meerkats time to hunt

(C) to sound a warning when enemies are spotted

(D) because they can stand up straight and tall

Read this story about the changing of the seasons. Then answer questions 1 through 4.

Autumn Dance

Every October, autumn bullies summer into letting go of the skies. The wind breathes a chill into the air. The sun gets tired and goes to bed earlier each night, and night sleeps in later each day. The trees dress in bright gowns for the last celebration of the season, and the leaves are skipping and dancing down the sidewalk. This is autumn, standing firm with hands on her hips, until winter peers over the edge of the world.

1. **This passage mostly tells about —**

(A) winter turning into spring.

(B) fall turning into winter.

(C) spring turning into summer.

(D) summer turning into fall.

2. **How does the sun change during autumn?**

(F) It rises and sets earlier than in the summer.

(G) It rises and sets later than in the summer.

(H) It rises later but sets earlier than in the summer.

(J) It rises earlier but sets later than in the summer.

3. **What is the author referring to when she describes the trees dressed in "bright gowns"?**

(A) leaves that have changed color but have not yet fallen from the trees

(B) green leaves

(C) formal dresses

(D) the trees' empty branches

4. **Personification means "giving human qualities to animals or objects." Which sentence is not an example of personification?**

(F) Every October, autumn bullies summer into letting go of the skies.

(G) A cold wind blows.

(H) The leaves skipped and danced down the sidewalk.

(J) The sun gets tired and goes to bed.

GO ON

49

Read this story about an interesting plant. Then answer questions 5 through 10 on page 51.

Tough Tumbleweed

I'm a travelling tumbleweed, rolling along the dusty trails of the wild, wild West. Well, actually I'm blowing across somebody's backyard in suburban Texas. These days it's hard to find a large open space. Back in the good old days, my ancestors tumbled across miles and miles of deserts or plains. Today, it's hard to find a mile without a strip mall or housing complex. Life for tumbleweeds just isn't that exciting anymore.

My great-great-great grandfather was one of the first immigrants to America. He sneaked into the country with a load of wheat from Russia. He and the other tumbleweeds used to be called Russian thistle before they came to America. Tumbleweeds are able to live on very little water, so my ancestors were able to spread across dry western lands that previously couldn't support plants. When a tumbleweed matures, it becomes dry and brittle. A strong wind comes along and—snap!— off it goes, tumbling across the landscape. As it rolls, it drops seeds in new places.

My family has had many adventures over the years. My great-great uncle tumbled with Crazy Horse, the legendary American Indian. My great-grandmother tumbled with the covered wagons. My father even tumbled on the set of a Hollywood western movie.

But, modern times are not as kind to us tumbleweeds. We get caught in fences and ditches. Our worst enemy is the automobile. My cousin was trapped under a car and caught fire from the heat of the muffler. He became a tumbleweed torch! Some people hate us tumbleweeds and try to burn us up. They can burn all they want, because tumbleweeds are not in danger of becoming extinct. We will be around for a long, long time. Our species wouldn't have lasted this long if we weren't stubborn. We've learned to adapt to civilization and to deal with humans who have taken over our land.

Tumbleweeds aren't called tough for nothing!

5. **What is the main idea of this story?**
   - (A) how tumbleweeds have been used throughout history
   - (B) how tumbleweeds survive and how modern times have affected them
   - (C) how people feel about tumbleweeds
   - (D) how tumbleweeds are used in Hollywood movies

6. **Tumbleweeds came to America from —**
   - (F) Russia.
   - (G) Texas.
   - (H) Hollywood.
   - (J) the West.

7. **How does the narrator of this story feel?**
   - (A) He is happy with modern inventions.
   - (B) He longs for the days when there were more wide-open spaces.
   - (C) He appreciates the need for housing complexes.
   - (D) He wishes he could be in a Hollywood movie.

8. **Which of these sentences is an opinion?**
   - (F) Tumbleweeds used to be called Russian thistle.
   - (G) Tumbleweeds are not in danger of becoming extinct.
   - (H) Tumbleweeds are able to live on very little water.
   - (J) Life for tumbleweeds just isn't that exciting anymore.

9. **The narrator in this story is —**
   - (A) a covered wagon.
   - (B) an American Indian.
   - (C) a tumbleweed.
   - (D) a Russian immigrant.

10. **What would be a good word to describe tumbleweed?**
    - (F) hardy
    - (G) fragile
    - (H) irritable
    - (J) delicate

GO ON

Name _____ Date_____

Read the story. Then answer questions 11 through 16 on page 53.

Pocahontas

There lived in Virginia in the early 1600s a beautiful girl named Pocahontas. Her name meant *Playful One*. She was the daughter of Powhatan, the chief of some 30 Indian tribes in Virginia.

Pocahontas is remembered for saving the life of Captain John Smith. Smith was the leader of the Jamestown colony founded by the English in 1607. In that same year, he was captured by the Indians and sentenced to death by Chief Powhatan. According to Smith's own account, he was ordered to lay his head on large stones in anticipation of being clubbed to death by several braves. At this point, Pocahontas is said to have knelt beside the Englishman and placed her head on his. Powhatan was apparently touched by this gesture, and he ordered that Smith be set free.

It is not certain if the above story is true. What casts doubt on its validity is that Smith later claimed to have been saved in the same manner by an Indian girl in New Hampshire.

Regardless, Pocahontas was a real person who did much to improve relations between her people and the English settlers. After the Smith incident, it was mostly peaceful between the two peoples until Powhatan's death in 1618.

In 1613, Pocahontas was captured and held hostage by the English. During her year of captivity, she met and married John Rolfe, a Virginia tobacco planter. In 1616, she accompanied Rolfe to England, where she was presented at the royal court. Pocahontas died there of smallpox in 1617, shortly before her planned return to America. She was buried at Gravesend, England.

John Rolfe returned to Virginia where he died in 1622. Thomas, the son of Rolfe and Pocahontas, later became a distinguished Virginian. Today, a number of Virginian families claim to be descendants of Pocahontas and John Rolfe.

GO ON

11. **Which of the following would make a good title for this story?**

　(A) Chief Powhatan and His Thirty Tribes

　(B) The Capture of John Smith

　(C) The Life of Pocahontas

　(D) Life on a Virginia Tobacco Farm

Here is a sequence of events that happened in the story.

| Pocahontas improved relations between her tribe and the English. |
| The English captured Pocahontas. |
| |
| Pocahontas traveled to England. |

12. **Which of these events should go in the empty box?**

　(F) Chief Powhatan died.

　(G) Pocahontas married John Rolfo.

　(H) Pocahontas saved John Smith.

　(J) John Rolfe was killed.

13. **Why do some people think John Smith's story about being saved by Pocahontas is not true?**

　(A) because John Rolfe also claimed he was rescued by Pocahontas

　(B) because Pocahontas was not a real person

　(C) because there were no witnesses

　(D) because he said the same thing happened to him with another tribe

14. **How did Pocahontas die?**

　(F) She died of smallpox.

　(G) She was clubbed to death.

　(H) She was killed during an Indian uprising.

　(J) She drowned on her way to England.

15. **In this story, you learn the most about —**

　(A) Powhatan.

　(B) John Rolfe.

　(C) Pocahontas.

　(D) John Smith.

16. **The people who claim to be descendants of Pocahontas and John Rolfe are probably —**

　(F) members of an historical society.

　(G) proud of their heritage.

　(H) ashamed by their family history.

　(J) good storytellers.

READING PRACTICE TEST
Part 2: Comprehension (cont.)

Here is a story about a very unusual animal. Read the story and then answer questions 17 through 20.

Mammal, Fish, or Fowl?

When scientists in England received reports from Australia about the duckbill platypus in the late 1700s, they thought they were the victims of a hoax. Surely, they must have reasoned, some jokester had sewn body parts from several different animals together in an attempt to trick them.

Indeed, the duckbill platypus is a strange animal. It has a bill resembling a duck; a flat, paddle-shaped tail like a beaver; and the shuffling gait of an alligator. Both its front and hind feet are webbed and have claws. Unlike most mammals, it has neither lips nor exterior ears. Although it nurses its young, it does not give birth to live babies. Instead it lays eggs—like a chicken! Small wonder that scientists were confused and not certain whether they were dealing with fish, fowl, or some kind of new species. They eventually classified the platypus with mammals.

17. This story mostly describes —
- (A) why scientists decided that the platypus was a mammal.
- (B) the unique features of the platypus.
- (C) where the platypus can be found.
- (D) a scientific hoax.

18. Which of the following statements is false?
- (F) The platypus has a tail that resembles a beaver's tail.
- (G) English scientists first learned about the platypus in the late 1700s.
- (H) The platypus does not have lips.
- (J) The platypus is a type of bird.

19. Which sentence is probably true?
- (A) One scientist probably made the decision on how the platypus would be classified.
- (B) Scientists were probably in complete agreement on how to classify the platypus.
- (C) Scientists probably debated over how the platypus should be classified.
- (D) Scientists probably let the people of England vote on how the platypus should be classified.

20. Which of these characteristics would have helped the scientists decide that the platypus was a mammal?
- (F) The platypus nurses its young.
- (G) The platypus lays eggs.
- (H) The platypus does not have external ears.
- (J) The platypus has a bill like a duck.

LANGUAGE: MECHANICS

● Lesson 1: Punctuation

Directions: Fill in the circle next to the punctuation mark that is needed in the sentence. Fill in the space for "None" if no additional punctuation marks are needed.

Examples

A. No I wasn't late for practice.

- (A) ;
- (B) ,
- (C) "
- (D) None

B. The coach said, "The game will start in about an hour."

- (F) "
- (G) ?
- (H) .
- (J) None

 Clue Read each sentence carefully. Pay special attention to the punctuation marks that are shown.

● Practice

1. The team carried in the bats balls, and gloves.
   - (A) ;
   - (B) ,
   - (C) :
   - (D) None

2. "Great catch" yelled the pitcher.
   - (F) ?
   - (G) .
   - (H) !
   - (J) None

3. Did you see that foul ball
   - (A) ?
   - (B) .
   - (C) ,
   - (D) None

4. Matilda hit a home run.
   - (F) !
   - (G) "
   - (H) ,
   - (J) None

5. That's three strikes," said the umpire.
   - (A) ,
   - (B) "
   - (C) "
   - (D) None

6. Yes the Fifth Grade Firecrackers won the game.
   - (F) ,
   - (G) .
   - (H) !
   - (J) None

STOP

LANGUAGE: MECHANICS

● Lesson 2: Punctuation

Directions: For A and questions 1–5, read each item. Fill in the circle next to the choice that has a punctuation error. If there is no mistake, fill in the fourth answer choice.

Example

A.
- (A) Samuel Clemens moved west
- (B) because he wanted to,
- (C) strike it rich in the mines.
- (D) No mistakes

 Remember, you are looking for the answer that shows a punctuation mistake.

● Practice

1.
- (A) Samuel Clemens had no money
- (B) He began writing articles
- (C) for a newspaper called the *Territorial Enterprises.*
- (D) No mistakes

2.
- (F) Samuel's newspaper articles
- (G) were eventually compiled
- (H) into his first book, Roughing It
- (J) No mistakes

3.
- (A) Samuel Clemens
- (B) first used the pen name:
- (C) Mark Twain while he worked as a writer in Virginia City, Nevada.
- (D) No mistakes

4.
- (F) 742 West Main Street
- (G) Virginia City, NV, 80235
- (H) December 12, 2003
- (J) No mistakes

5.
- (A) Dear Mr. Pendleton,
- (B) Thank you for telling our class about Mark Twain.
- (C) He was a real character?
- (D) No mistakes

For numbers 6 and 7, read each sentence with a blank. Choose the word or words that fit best in the blank and show the correct punctuation.

6. Gabriel watched a caterpillar climb up the side of _____ aquarium.
- (F) its
- (G) it's
- (H) its'
- (J) its's

7. He placed bits of grass, _____ small twigs inside.
- (A) some lettuce and
- (B) some lettuce, and
- (C) some lettuce, and,
- (D) some lettuce and,

Name _____ Date_____

LANGUAGE: MECHANICS

● Lesson 3: Capitalization and Punctuation

Directions: For A and numbers 1–2, choose the answer that shows correct punctuation. For B and numbers 3–5, choose the answer that shows correct punctuation of the underlined part. Fill in the circle for "Correct as it is" if the underlined part is correct.

Examples

A.
- Ⓐ "Where is your suntan lotion," Debbie asked Veronica.
- Ⓑ "Oh, I dont use that," veronica told her. "I want a great tan."
- Ⓒ "That's not a great idea," Debbie said, shaking her head.
- Ⓓ "We'll be outside from noon until 3:00.'

B. The <u>statue of Liberty</u> is one of the best known symbols in the United States.
- Ⓕ Statue of Liberty
- Ⓖ statue of liberty
- Ⓗ Statue of liberty
- Ⓙ Correct as it is

 Clue To narrow your choices, eliminate answers you know for sure are incorrect.

● Practice

1.
- Ⓐ In the years following the civil war Chicago became the railroad and commercial center in America.
- Ⓑ With business thriving, no one was prepared for what happened on October 8, 1871.
- Ⓒ A fire broke out in the Lumber District.
- Ⓓ The fire was one of the worst fires in u.s. history.

2.
- Ⓕ Crocodiles are on every continent except europe and antarctica.
- Ⓖ Alligators except for a species native to eastern China are limited to the United States.
- Ⓗ Alligators inhabit Swamps, Rivers, and Coastal Areas of many southern states.
- Ⓙ The best way to tell a crocodile from an alligator is by observing its snout.

3. On December 7, 1941, Japanese planes attacked the U.S. naval base at <u>Pearl Harbor, Hawaii.</u>
- Ⓐ Pearl Harbor Hawaii
- Ⓑ Pearl, Harbor, Hawaii
- Ⓒ pearl harbor, Hawaii
- Ⓓ Correct as it is

4. Many acts of heroism <u>were recorded, in the hours</u> following the attack.
- Ⓕ were recorded; in the hours
- Ⓖ were recorded in the hours
- Ⓗ were recorded in the hours,
- Ⓙ Correct as it is

5. An army <u>pilot, lieutenant George Bickell was one</u> man honored for his heroics.
- Ⓐ pilot, lieutenant George Bickell,
- Ⓑ pilot Lieutenant George Bickell
- Ⓒ pilot, Lieutenant George Bickell,
- Ⓓ Correct as it is

 STOP

LANGUAGE: MECHANICS

● Lesson 4: Capitalization and Punctuation

Directions: Read the passage. Fill in the circle for the answer that shows the correct punctuation and capitalization for the underlined word or words. Fill in the circle for "Correct as it is" if the underlined part is correct.

Example

Rock and roll originally began in the 1950s. It was the first music that American teenagers could claim as <u>their own its themes</u> were centered around dances, cars, and relationships. And it was simple and easy to remember.

A.
- Ⓐ their own. Its themes
- Ⓑ their own. It's themes
- Ⓒ their own, its themes
- Ⓓ Correct as it is

 Clue Answer the easiest questions first. Then go back to the harder questions.

● Practice

The cowboys of the Pecos River region were a rough and fearsome **(1)** <u>lot it</u> was only natural that **(2)** <u>theyd</u> invent a character like Pecos Bill. **(3)** <u>Bills talents</u> allowed him to do many things. Among his exploits, he ended a long drought in Texas by digging the **(4)** <u>rio grande river</u> to get water from the Gulf of Mexico. **(5)** <u>On another occasion,</u> Bill rode a cyclone without a saddle until it "rained out" from under him. The resulting downpour created the Grand Canyon. Bill was also credited with inventing roping and other skills important to cowboys. After becoming a cowboy, he rode a wild horse **(6)** <u>named "Widow Maker".</u>

1.
- Ⓐ lot? It
- Ⓑ lot, it
- Ⓒ lot. It
- Ⓓ Correct as it is

2.
- Ⓕ they'd
- Ⓖ they'ld
- Ⓗ theyd'
- Ⓙ Correct as it is

3.
- Ⓐ Bills' talents
- Ⓑ Bill's talents
- Ⓒ Bills talent's
- Ⓓ Correct as it is

4.
- Ⓕ Rio Grande river
- Ⓖ Rio Grande River
- Ⓗ rio grande River
- Ⓙ Correct as it is

5.
- Ⓐ On another occasion:
- Ⓑ On another occasion;
- Ⓒ On another occasion.
- Ⓓ Correct as it is

6.
- Ⓕ named Widow Maker.
- Ⓖ named "Widow Maker."
- Ⓗ named, "Widow Maker."
- Ⓙ Correct as it is

LANGUAGE: MECHANICS

● Lesson 5: Capitalization and Punctuation

Directions: Read the sentence with a blank. Fill in the circle for the answer choice that best fits in the blank and has correct capitalization and punctuation.

Examples

A. "How did you win so _____ asked.

- Ⓐ easily," They
- Ⓑ easily?" they
- Ⓒ easily" they
- Ⓓ easily!" They

B. My _____ gnawed happily on his bone.

- Ⓕ friends's dog
- Ⓖ Friends' dog
- Ⓗ Friend's dog
- Ⓙ friend's dog

Clue Remember to look for the answer that shows both correct capitalization and punctuation.

● Practice

1. **School is in session from ____**
   - Ⓐ september through june!
   - Ⓑ September, through June.
   - Ⓒ September through June?
   - Ⓓ September through June.

2. **We took a tour of ____ office.**
   - Ⓕ Dr. Eli Hansen's
   - Ⓖ Dr Eli Hansens'
   - Ⓗ Dr. Eli Hansens
   - Ⓙ dr. Eli Hansen's

3. **The waiter ____ I get you anything else?"**
   - Ⓐ "Asked can
   - Ⓑ asked, "Can
   - Ⓒ asked. "Can
   - Ⓓ asked "Can

4. **Pamela takes ____ lessons after school.**
   - Ⓕ Piano lessons, Art lessons, and Dance
   - Ⓖ piano lessons art lessons and dance
   - Ⓗ piano lessons, art lessons, and dance
   - Ⓙ piano, lessons, art, lessons, and dance,

5. **The ____ of students at my school is 48 inches.**
   - Ⓐ Average Height
   - Ⓑ average height
   - Ⓒ average height,
   - Ⓓ Average height

6. **I was surprised by what I had ____ would ever believe me.**
   - Ⓕ found; No one
   - Ⓖ found? No one
   - Ⓗ found, no one
   - Ⓙ found. No one

7. **I am interested in buying stickers, ____ the best.**
   - Ⓐ and yours are
   - Ⓑ and your's are
   - Ⓒ and yours' are
   - Ⓓ and yours, are

8. **The people who live on ____ about the noise from the nearby airport.**
   - Ⓕ Grant street complain
   - Ⓖ Grant Street. Complain
   - Ⓗ grant street complain
   - Ⓙ Grant Street complain

STOP

LANGUAGE: MECHANICS

● **Lesson 6: Titles, Introductory Elements, Direct Address**

Directions: Choose the sentence with correct punctuation.

Examples

A.
- (A) At twelve o'clock the doorbell, rang.
- (B) At twelve o'clock, the doorbell rang.
- (C) At twelve, o'clock, the doorbell rang.
- (D) At twelve, o'clock the doorbell, rang.

B.
- (F) Yes dear you can go to Joe's house.
- (G) Yes dear, you can go to Joe's, house.
- (H) Yes, dear, you can go to Joe's house.
- (J) Yes dear, you can go, to Joe's house.

● Practice

1.
- (A) I loved the book The History of Dogs.
- (B) I loved the book "The History of Dogs."
- (C) I loved the book *The History of Dogs.*
- (D) I loved the book The history of dogs.

2.
- (F) My favorite song is "Over the Rainbow."
- (G) My favorite song is Over the Rainbow.
- (H) My favorite song is over the rainbow.
- (J) My favorite song is Over the Rainbow.

3.
- (A) Let's go see the movie *Titanic.*
- (B) Let's go see the movie "Titanic."
- (C) Let's go see the movie Titanic.
- (D) Let's go see the movie titanic.

4.
- (F) At the zoo, we saw lions and tigers and bears.
- (G) At the zoo we saw lions and tigers and, bears.
- (H) At the zoo we saw, lions and tigers and bears.
- (J) At the zoo, we saw, lions, and tigers, and bears.

5.
- (A) Is it true are Mark and Jason coming to the party?
- (B) Is it, true are Mark and Jason coming to the party?
- (C) Is it true are Mark, and Jason, coming to the party?
- (D) Is it true, are Mark and Jason coming to the party?

6.
- (F) Is that correct, Sam?
- (G) Is that correct Sam?
- (H) Is that, correct Sam?
- (J) Is that, correct, Sam?

LANGUAGE: MECHANICS
SAMPLE TEST

Directions: Read the directions for each section. Fill in the circle for the correct answer.

Example

Fill in the circle next to the punctuation mark that is needed in the sentence.
Fill in the space for "None" if no additional punctuation marks are needed.

A. "You can see the Grand Canyon out of the left windows" announced the pilot.

- (F) ?
- (G) ,
- (H) .
- (J) None

For numbers 1–3, fill in the circle next to the punctuation mark that is needed in the sentence. Fill in the space for "None" if no additional punctuation marks are needed.

1. When we left the cafeteria this afternoon we headed for the library.
   - (A) ;
   - (B) ,
   - (C) .
   - (D) Nono

2. "Hey, Mitzi. Are you okay? asked Charles.
   - (F) "
   - (G) ,
   - (H) "
   - (J) None

3. "I'm King of the Mountain" cried Madeline.
   - (A) !
   - (B) .
   - (C) ?
   - (D) None

For numbers 4–6, fill in the circle next to the choice that has a punctuation error. If there is no mistake, fill in the fourth answer choice.

4.
   - (F) I cant finish
   - (G) the project, because
   - (H) I'm going on vacation.
   - (J) No mistakes

5.
   - (A) Yes, I'll go.
   - (B) I always enjoy a day
   - (C) at the park
   - (D) No mistakes

6.
   - (F) John still has to
   - (G) clear the table wash the dishes and wipe down the counters
   - (H) before he can watch television.
   - (J) No mistakes

For numbers 7 and 8, read each sentence. Fill in the circle for the answer choice that best fits in the blank and has correct capitalization and punctuation.

7. I like to play _____ I like basketball even better.
   - (A) baseball, but,
   - (B) baseball but,
   - (C) baseball. But
   - (D) baseball, but

GO ON

61

LANGUAGE: MECHANICS
SAMPLE TEST (cont.)

8. The _____ were lined up for miles, and not one of them was moving.

(F) cars's

(G) cars

(H) cars'

(J) car's

For numbers 9–12, read each group of sentences. Fill in the circle next to the sentence that is written correctly and shows the correct capitalization and punctuation.

9. (A) Jake and Tristan went to the movies

(B) They paid for their tickets popcorn and sodas.

(C) They watched the previews?

(D) When the movie started, they stopped talking.

10. (F) Los Angeles, California, is a favorite vacation spot.

(G) People come to see the Beaches, Amusement Parks, and Movie Studios.

(H) Some people like to find celebrity homes in beverly hills.

(J) The hollywood sign, is a famous landmark.

11. (A) Native americans used stories to tell about nature and the world.

(B) The Cherokees have a legend about how fire came to Earth.

(C) A bolt of lightning struck a Sycamore Tree on an island.

(D) A water spider, carried a chunk of coal, across the water, to the mainland.

12. (F) The underground, railroad helped runaway slaves escape to freedom.

(G) Railroad terminology was used as a type of code to confuse the Slave Catchers.

(H) People who hid slaves in their homes were called "stationmasters."

(J) People who escorted the runaway slaves along the escape routes were called "conductors?"

For numbers 13–16, read the sentence. Fill in the circle for the answer choice that best fits in the blank and has correct capitalization and punctuation.

13. _____ is taking a cooking class on Saturdays.

(A) Mr. Duncan, my teacher

(B) Mr. Duncan, my teacher,

(C) Mr. Duncan my teacher

(D) Mr. Duncan, my Teacher

14. **Someday, I would like to go to _____**

(F) Hawaii.

(G) hawaii,

(H) Hawaii?

(J) hawaii.

15. **The house at 609 Lucia _____ is getting a new roof.**

(A) AVE

(B) AVE.

(C) Ave

(D) Ave.

GO ON

16. _____ that view beautiful?

  (F) Isnt'
  (G) Isnt
  (H) Isn't
  (J) Is'nt

For numbers 17–20, look at the underlined part of each sentence. Fill in the circle for the answer choice that shows correct punctuation and capitalization. Fill in the circle for "Correct as it is" if the underlined part is correct.

17. Many times, the <u>earths plates</u> move along an existing fault.

  (A) earths' plates
  (B) earths's plates
  (C) earth's plates
  (D) Correct as it is

18. "I wonder if people in the Middle Ages had pet <u>dogs" Brian</u> said.

  (F) dogs." Brian
  (G) dogs," Brian
  (H) dogs?" Brian
  (J) Correct as it is

19. Saguaro cacti live in one of <u>the hottest driest</u> parts of North America.

  (A) the hottest, driest
  (B) the hottest, driest,
  (C) the, hottest, driest
  (D) Correct as it is

20. The primary colors of pigments are <u>red blue and yellow</u>

  (F) red, blue and yellow?
  (G) red blue, and yellow.
  (H) red, blue, and yellow.
  (J) Correct as it is

For numbers 21–24, fill in the circle for the answer that shows the correct punctuation and capitalization for the underlined word or words.

Firefighters work day and night. When there is a **(21)** <u>fire each</u> firefighter has a special duty. The duty may be to **(22)** <u>connect hoses to Water Hydrants</u>, set up ladders, look for and rescue people, break windows, or cut holes in the roof or walls of the building to let smoke, gas, and heat escape. When **(23)** <u>firefighters</u> are not fighting fires, they clean and maintain their equipment. They attend classes and have practice drills so they can bocome better **(24)** <u>firefighters, also</u> they exercise to stay in shape.

21. (A) a fire. Each
     (B) a fire, each
     (C) a fire; each
     (D) Correct as it is

22. (F) connect hoses, to water hydrants
     (G) connect hoses to water hydrants.
     (H) connect hoses to water hydrants
     (J) Correct as it is

23. (A) Firefighters
     (B) firefighters'
     (C) firefighter's
     (D) Correct as it is

24. (F) firefighters. Also,
     (G) firefighters, also,
     (H) firefighters! Also
     (J) Correct as it is

This is a report about mountain forests. Read the report and use it to do numbers 25–28.

(1) The lower and middle slopes of a mountain are usually forest areas. (2) Coniferous forests have trees like Pines and Spruces. (3) These trees have leaves shaped like needles that stay green all year. (4) Deciduous forests have trees like oaks and maples. (5) These tree's have broad leaves that change colors and fall off in autumn. (6) The trees serve as homes for many birds and rodents. (7) Forest predators stalk their prey among the trees. (8) The forest area comes to an end at a point called the timberline. (9) This is the point beyond which it is too cold. for trees to grow.

25. **In sentence 2, Pines and Spruces. is best written —**
    - (A) pines and spruces?
    - (B) pines and spruces.
    - (C) Pines and Spruces;
    - (D) As it is

26. **In sentence 5, These tree's is best written —**
    - (F) These trees
    - (G) These trees's
    - (H) These trees'
    - (J) As it is

27. **In sentence 6, many birds and rodents. is best written —**
    - (A) many, birds, and rodents.
    - (B) many birds and, rodents.
    - (C) many birds, and rodents.
    - (D) As it is

28. **In sentence 9, too cold. for trees is best written —**
    - (F) too cold, for trees
    - (G) too cold for trees
    - (H) too cold. For trees
    - (J) As it is

STOP

LANGUAGE: EXPRESSION

● Lesson 7: Usage

Directions: Choose the word or phrase that best completes the sentence.

Examples

A. They _____ only two days to go until the science fair.

- (A) hads
- (B) haves
- (C) had
- (D) half

B. She _____ if she could go to the play.

- (F) axed
- (G) asked
- (H) asking
- (J) ask

Clue If you are not sure which answer is correct, try each one in the blank. Choose the one that sounds best.

● Practice

1. Jeremy taught _____ to play the guitar.
   - (A) hisself
   - (B) itself
   - (C) themselves
   - (D) himself

2. The sleek steamer _____ through the quiet night.
   - (F) slided
   - (G) slipped
   - (H) slipping
   - (J) sliding

3. The dog _____ under the fence.
   - (A) crawled
   - (B) to crawl
   - (C) crawling
   - (D) crawlings

4. Tomorrow, I _____ my friend.
   - (F) to meet
   - (G) will meet
   - (H) meets
   - (J) met

5. Sheila is _____ than I am.
   - (A) more hungrier
   - (B) hungriest
   - (C) most hungry
   - (D) hungrier

6. The twins can take care of _____ .
   - (F) themselves
   - (G) herself
   - (H) himself
   - (J) yourselves

7. The roses _____ than the carnations.
   - (A) are more fragranter
   - (B) is more fragrant
   - (C) was more fragrant
   - (D) were more fragrant

8. He was the _____ member of the club.
   - (F) more louder
   - (G) louder
   - (H) loudest
   - (J) most loud

STOP

LANGUAGE: EXPRESSION

● Lesson 8: Usage

Directions: Read the directions for each section. Fill in the circle for the correct answer.

Examples

Choose the answer that is a complete and correctly written sentence.

A.
- (A) The club members met in its treehouse.
- (B) Each week, thems had a meeting.
- (C) They chose Reggie as the club president.
- (D) Reggie builded the treehouse.

Read each answer choice. Fill in the circle for the choice that has an error. If there are no errors, fill in the fourth circle.

B.
- (F) A ample supply of
- (G) fruits and vegetables
- (H) is needed for a healthy diet.
- (J) No mistakes

Clue Look carefully at all of the answer choices before you choose the one you think is correct.

● Practice

For numbers 1–2, choose the answer that is a complete and correctly written sentence.

1.
- (A) Scientists spends many hours recording the behavior and habits of animals.
- (B) They search for clues to explain why animals act as they do.
- (C) Through careful observation, the behavior of an animal might could be explained.
- (D) Lemmings, however, does an unexplainable thing.

2.
- (F) Glass snakes ain't snakes at all.
- (G) They is one of several kinds of lizards that inhabitate the earth.
- (H) Most legless lizards resemble worms, but the glass snake looks very much like a true snake.
- (J) It can break off his tail as easily as a pieces of glass.

For numbers 3–5, read each answer choice. Fill in the circle for the choice that has an error. If there are no errors, fill in the fourth circle.

3.
- (A) A beach vacation and a ski vacation
- (B) is alike in some ways
- (C) and different in others.
- (D) No mistakes

4.
- (F) Doing the laundry is a big contribution
- (G) to my family, and I get to put away
- (H) my own clothes exactly the way I like them.
- (J) No mistakes

5.
- (A) For many years,
- (B) jigsaw puzzles have been entertained
- (C) to both children and adults.
- (D) No mistakes

LANGUAGE: EXPRESSION

● Lesson 9: Usage

Directions: Read each passage. Use the passage to answer the questions.

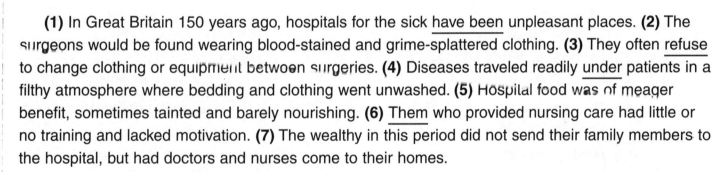

Example

(1) We was reading an article called "Food for Thought." (2) It is about what we should and shouldn't eat as snacks. (3) Some of the ideas in the article are very good, such as choosing an apple instead of chips. (4) The article makes me think, but it also makes me hungry.

A.   In sentence 1, We was is best written —

   A   We are

   B   We wasn't

   C   We is

   D   As it is

Read the underlined phrases carefully. Think of the best way to write those phrases.

● Practice

(1) In Great Britain 150 years ago, hospitals for the sick have been unpleasant places. (2) The surgeons would be found wearing blood-stained and grime-splattered clothing. (3) They often refuse to change clothing or equipment between surgeries. (4) Diseases traveled readily under patients in a filthy atmosphere where bedding and clothing went unwashed. (5) Hospital food was of meager benefit, sometimes tainted and barely nourishing. (6) Them who provided nursing care had little or no training and lacked motivation. (7) The wealthy in this period did not send their family members to the hospital, but had doctors and nurses come to their homes.

1.   **In sentence 1, have been is best written as —**

   A   were

   B   was

   C   are

   D   As it is

2.   **In sentence 3, refuse is best written —**

   F   refused

   G   refuses

   H   refusing

   J   As it is

3.   **In sentence 4, under is best written —**

   A   around

   B   through

   C   between

   D   As it is

4.   **In sentence 6, Them is best written —**

   F   Those

   G   They

   H   Themselves

   J   As it is

STOP

LANGUAGE: EXPRESSION

● Lesson 10: Verb Tenses

Directions: Choose the correct sentence.

Examples

A.
- (A) We will go to the fair, and we will see the animals.
- (B) We went to the fair, and we will see the animals.
- (C) We will go to the fair, and we saw the animals.
- (D) We go to the fair, and we saw the animals.

B.
- (F) They went on vacation later in the summer.
- (G) They going on vacation later in the summer.
- (H) They will go on vacation later in the summer.
- (J) They goes on vacation later in the summer.

● Practice

1.
- (A) Last week, Jenna and I had lunch at the restaurant.
- (B) Last week, Jenna and I have lunch at the restaurant.
- (C) Last week, Jenna and I has lunch at the restaurant.
- (D) Last week, Jenna and I will have lunch at the restaurant.

2.
- (F) Next week, Jenna and I had lunch at the diner.
- (G) Next week, Jenna and I having lunch at the diner.
- (H) Next week, Jenna and I has lunch at the diner.
- (J) Next week, Jenna and I will have lunch at the diner.

3.
- (A) Mia and Emmett will get married last Saturday.
- (B) Mia and Emmett got married last Saturday.
- (C) Mia and Emmett get married last Saturday.
- (D) Mia and Emmett should get married last Saturday.

4.
- (F) My dad has walked to school every day when he was young.
- (G) My dad had walked to school every day when he was young.
- (H) My dad will walk to school every day when he was young.
- (J) My dad have walk to school every day when he was young.

5.
- (A) Lucy bought five books, and I buy three books.
- (B) Lucy buys five books, and I bought three books.
- (C) Lucy bought five books, and I bought three books.
- (D) Lucy will buy five books, and I buying three books.

6.
- (F) I have biked twenty miles by the end of next week.
- (G) I had biked twenty miles by the end of next week.
- (H) I would have biking twenty miles by the end of next week.
- (J) I will have biked twenty miles by the end of next week.

STOP

LANGUAGE: EXPRESSION

● Lesson 11: Conjunctions, Prepositions, Interjections

Directions: Choose the correct sentence.

Examples

A.
- (A) Hang the picture through the table.
- (B) Hang the picture over the table.
- (C) Hang the picture within the table.
- (D) Hang the picture among the table.

B.
- (F) Why, here you are!
- (G) Why here you are!
- (H) Why! here you are.
- (J) Why here, you are!

● Practice

1.
- (A) Only one boy can win the contest, so it will be Henry and Luke.
- (B) Only one boy can win the contest, so it will be Henry nor Luke.
- (C) Only one boy can win the contest, so it will be Henry but Luke.
- (D) Only one boy can win the contest, so it will be Henry or Luke.

2.
- (F) The cat likes to sleep under the window where it is sunny.
- (G) The cat likes to sleep on top of the window where it is sunny.
- (H) The cat likes to sleep over the window where it is sunny.
- (J) The cat likes to sleep away from the window where it is sunny.

3.
- (A) All the girls or the boys is invited to the dance.
- (B) All the girls nor the boys are invited to the dance.
- (C) All the girls and the boys are invited to the dance.
- (D) All the girls but the boys are invited to the dance.

4.
- (F) I walked up the sidewalk, either I did not go into the house.
- (G) I walked up the sidewalk, or I did not go into the house.
- (H) I walked up the sidewalk, but I did not go into the house.
- (J) I walked up the sidewalk, nor I did not go into the house.

5.
- (A) Hey it's my turn next!
- (B) Hey, it's my turn next!
- (C) Hey! it's my turn next.
- (D) Hey it's, my turn next!

6.
- (F) Either Nick and Brayden wants chocolate ice cream.
- (G) Either Nick nor Brayden wants chocolate ice cream.
- (H) Neither Nick or Brayden wants chocolate ice cream.
- (J) Neither Nick nor Brayden wants chocolate ice cream.

LANGUAGE: EXPRESSION

● Lesson 12: Sentences

Directions: Read the directions for each section. Fill in the circle for the correct answer.

Examples

Find the underlined part that is the simple subject of the sentence.

A. The <u>cat</u> <u>jumped</u> from the <u>bed</u> to the <u>floor</u>.
       Ⓐ   Ⓑ   Ⓒ   Ⓓ

Find the underlined part that is the simple predicate (verb) of the sentence.

B. <u>Joshua</u> <u>painted</u> a <u>picture</u> of the <u>mountains</u>.
       Ⓕ   Ⓖ   Ⓗ   Ⓙ

 Clue Read each sentence carefully. Decide who the sentence is about and what action is taking place.

● Practice

For numbers 1–3, find the underlined part that is the simple subject of the sentence.

1. <u>My</u> <u>dad</u> <u>cooked</u> <u>spaghetti and meatballs</u> for dinner.
   Ⓐ Ⓑ Ⓒ   Ⓓ

2. <u>Last</u> <u>year</u>, <u>we</u> were in fourth <u>grade</u>.
   Ⓕ   Ⓖ Ⓗ   Ⓙ

3. The <u>team</u> <u>celebrated</u> its <u>victory</u> at the <u>pizza</u> parlor.
     Ⓐ   Ⓑ   Ⓒ   Ⓓ

For numbers 4–6, find the underlined part that is the simple predicate (verb) of the sentence.

4. <u>Ramona</u> <u>performed</u> a <u>dance</u> routine for the <u>talent</u> show.
    Ⓕ   Ⓖ   Ⓗ   Ⓙ

5. The <u>animals</u> at the <u>zoo</u> usually <u>eat</u> around sunset.
   Ⓐ   Ⓑ   Ⓒ Ⓓ

6. Often, <u>Eli</u> <u>delivers</u> his <u>packages</u> before <u>lunchtime</u>.
   Ⓕ Ⓖ   Ⓗ   Ⓙ

 GO ON

LANGUAGE: EXPRESSION

● Lesson 12: Sentences (cont.)

Directions: Choose the answer that best combines the underlined sentences.

Example

A. **Amber enjoys horseback riding.**

Amber enjoys soccer.

- (A) Amber enjoys horseback riding, but also soccer.
- (B) Soccer and horseback riding are enjoyed by Amber.
- (C) Amber enjoys horseback riding and soccer.
- (D) Amber enjoys soccer but not horseback riding.

 Clue Read each answer choice carefully. Decide which one sounds the best.

● Practice

7. **The computer is working.**
   I can't connect to the Internet.

   - (A) I can't connect to the Internet if the computer is working.
   - (B) I can't connect to the Internet with the computer.
   - (C) The computer is working, so I can't connect to the Internet.
   - (D) The computer is working, but I can't connect to the Internet.

8. **We raked the leaves yesterday.**
   The wind blew the leaves off the trees.

   - (F) Yesterday, we raked the leaves that the wind blew off the trees.
   - (G) The wind blew the leaves up the trees, so we raked them up yesterday.
   - (H) The leaves, that we raked were blown.
   - (J) We raked the leaves yesterday and the wind blew the leaves off the trees.

9. **The lodge is over 200 years old.**
   The lodge is still a comfortable place to stay.

   - (A) The lodge, which is over 200 years old, is still a comfortable place to stay.
   - (B) Still a comfortable place to stay, the lodge is over 200 years old.
   - (C) The lodge is over 200 years old, because it is still a comfortable place to stay.
   - (D) Because it is over 200 years old, the lodge is still a comfortable place to stay.

STOP

LANGUAGE: EXPRESSION

● Lesson 13: Sentences

Directions: Choose the best way to express the idea. Fill in the circle for the correct answer.

Example

A.
- (A) Though once calm in the morning, the seas were choppy by afternoon.
- (B) The seas became choppy in the afternoon, and it was calm in the morning.
- (C) The seas were calm in the morning, but by the afternoon they had become choppy.
- (D) The seas were calm in the morning, because they were choppy in the afternoon.

 Clue If you are not sure which answer is correct, say each one to yourself. The correct answer will usually sound the best.

● Practice

Read the story. Use it to complete numbers 1–2.

(1) Last Saturday, the Wilson family drove to Chicago to watch a Cubs baseball game. (2) The bustling streets around the ballpark were filled with activity. (3) The children spotted a booth outside the stadium that was selling Cubs' baseball caps. (4) They begged their dad to buy each of them a hat. (5) He insisted that they wait until they got inside the park. (6) When they got to the front of the line, the children saw a woman handing out free Cubs' hats. (7) It was free hat day. (8) Mr. Wilson smiled and the children cheered.

1. How is sentence 1 best written?
- (A) On a drive to Chicago last Saturday, the Wilson family was watching a Cubs baseball game.
- (B) To watch a Cubs baseball game, the Wilson family drove to Chicago last Saturday.
- (C) Last Saturday, the Wilson family was driving to Chicago and watching a Cubs baseball game.
- (D) As it is

2. What is the best way to combine sentences 4 and 5 without changing their meaning?
- (F) They begged their dad to buy each of them a hat, but he insisted that they wait until they got inside the park.
- (G) They begged their dad to buy each of them a hat, because he insisted that they wait until they got inside the park.
- (H) They begged their dad to buy each of them a hat; therefore, he insisted that they wait until they got inside the park.
- (J) Since their dad insisted that they wait until they got inside the park, they begged him to buy each of them a hat.

 STOP

LANGUAGE: EXPRESSION

● Lesson 14: Paragraphs

Directions: For A and numbers 1–2, choose the best topic sentence for the paragraph.

Example

A. _____. Snails produce a liquid on the bottom of their feet. Then they "surf" on the rippling waves of this sticky liquid. Sea stars have slender tube feet with tiny suction cups that help them grip. Dolphins whip their tails up and down to thrust their bodies through the water.

- (A) Animals eat a variety of foods found in nature.
- (B) There are many different animals in the United States.
- (C) Animals move about in many unusual ways.
- (D) Animals have different kinds of feet.

 Clue A paragraph should be about one idea. The correct answer is the one that fits best with the rest of the paragraph.

● Practice

1. _____. A honeybee collects pollen and nectar from a flower. When the bee goes to the next flower, some of the pollen from the first flower falls onto the second. The second flower uses this pollen to make seeds.

- (A) It is estimated that honeybees pollinate billions of dollars worth of crops each year.
- (B) The most important role of the honeybee is to pollinate plants.
- (C) If you are stung by a bee, remove the stinger carefully.
- (D) Bees are considered pests.

2. _____. Toads and tree frogs croak in the evenings. Sometimes the chirping of the crickets is so loud that you can't hear the little frogs. But the booming of the big bullfrogs can always be heard. I don't know how Lane Roy sleeps.

- (F) Crickets are louder than frogs.
- (G) Swamps are homes to many different creatures.
- (H) Frogs make a variety of sounds.
- (J) The swamp behind the house is filled with sound.

For number 3, find the answer choice that best develops the topic sentence.

3. **Anne Frank was born into a prosperous German family.**

- (A) Her father, Otto, was a businessman. But the Franks were Jews and when Adolf Hitler took power, Otto moved his family to Amsterdam.
- (B) For two years, Anne and seven other people lived in a secret annex. They had to remain still and quiet during the day.
- (C) When Otto was released from the concentration camp, he returned to Amsterdam. He was the only person in his family who had survived.
- (D) Anne found comfort writing in her diary. She wrote about the cramped space she lived in, about the quarrels and difficulties of life in their hiding place, and about her fears and joys.

 STOP

LANGUAGE: EXPRESSION

● Lesson 15: Paragraphs

Directions: Read the paragraph. Fill in the circle next to the sentence that does not belong in the paragraph.

Example

A. **(1)** In 3000 B.C., the early Egyptian boats were constructed from the *papyrus* plant. **(2)** With the Egyptian's limited knowledge of navigation, they could only sail with the wind. **(3)** These reeds, from which early paper was made, could grow to be 20 feet high. **(4)** The reeds were cut, bundled, and tied together to form the boat.

- (A) Sentence 1
- (B) Sentence 2
- (C) Sentence 3
- (D) Sentence 4

● Practice

Read each paragraph carefully to determine which sentence does not fit the main topic.

1. **(1)** In 1567, Francis Drake, John Hawkins, and other English seamen were on a voyage. **(2)** They hoped to make a profit by selling smuggled goods to some of the Spanish colonies. **(3)** On their way back from their voyage, they stopped at a Mexican port. **(4)** By far, Drake is best known as the first Englishman to sail around the world.

- (A) Sentence 1
- (B) Sentence 2
- (C) Sentence 3
- (D) Sentence 4

2. **(1)** In his book *Over the Top of the World,* Will Steger relates the travels of his research party across the Arctic Ocean from Siberia to Canada in 1994. **(2)** With a team of 6 people and 33 dogs, Steger set out by dogsled to complete this daring mission. **(3)** Steger is a good writer. **(4)** Along the way,

the party would exchange dogsleds for canoe sleds because of the breaking ice packs.

- (F) Sentence 1
- (G) Sentence 2
- (H) Sentence 3
- (J) Sentence 4

3. **(1)** The "Great Zimbabwe" is one of many stone-walled fortresses built on the Zimbabwean plateau. **(2)** The Shona spoke a common Bantu language and all were herdsmen and farmers. **(3)** Researchers believe that the Shona people built this structure over a course of 400 years. **(4)** More than 18,000 people may have lived in the "Great Zimbabwe."

- (A) Sentence 1
- (B) Sentence 2
- (C) Sentence 3
- (D) Sentence 4

LANGUAGE: EXPRESSION

● Lesson 16: Paragraphs

Directions: Read each paragraph. Use the paragraph to answer the questions.

Example

Some people in South Africa keep meerkats as pets. They are convenient to have around the house when mice and rats are a problem.

A. **Which is the best last sentence?**

- (A) The meerkat eats plants.
- (B) Meerkats can stand as straight as boards.
- (C) Meerkats are not cats.
- (D) Meerkats seem capable of performing some of the same duties as working cats.

 Clue Think about the topic of the paragraph. Make sure that all the sentences you choose match the same topic.

● Practice

(1) Frogs are unique and interesting animals. (2) Frogs have narrow bodies and ridges down their backs. (3) They have large, round ear membranes and small teeth in their upper jaws. (4) Their long hind legs enable them to take long leaps. (5) A toad's short legs limit it to only short jumps. (6) Frogs have smooth, moist, soft skin. (7) Most frogs are water-dwellers.

1. **If another paragraph were added that told about toads, what would make a good first sentence for that paragraph?**
   - (A) Their ear membranes are smaller than frogs'.
   - (B) In contrast to frogs, toads have chubby bodies and ridges on their heads.
   - (C) Frogs are similar to toads in many ways.
   - (D) However, they lay their eggs in strings rather than clumps.

2. **Which sentence should be left out of this paragraph?**
   - (F) Sentence 3
   - (G) Sentence 4
   - (H) Sentence 5
   - (J) Sentence 6

3. **Choose the best last sentence for this paragraph.**
   - (A) They lay clumps of eggs in their watery habitat.
   - (B) Toads have no teeth.
   - (C) Frogs make a loud croaking sound.
   - (D) Most toads make their homes on land.

 STOP

LANGUAGE: EXPRESSION

● **Lesson 17: Paragraphs**

Directions: Read each paragraph. Use the paragraphs to answer the questions.

Example

I'm writing a report in school about the state of Illinois. I think some of the stories about our family moving there would make it more interesting. Can you tell me about the time Grandma lived on the farm?

A. **Who would be an appropriate person to send this letter to?**
- (A) a business owner
- (B) a state congressman
- (C) a travel agent
- (D) a relative

 Clue Think about the request that is being made in each paragraph. Decide who would most likely be able to help fulfill the request.

● **Practice**

My family is planning a trip to Chicago, Illinois. We will arrive on July 1, and we plan to stay for five nights. Can you please help us find a hotel? Also, any information you can share about things to do in Chicago would be appreciated.

1. **Who would be an appropriate person to send this letter to?**
- (A) the owner of a restaurant
- (B) the mayor of Chicago
- (C) a hotel manager
- (D) a travel agent

2. **What needed information is missing from this letter?**
- (F) the number of nights the family will be staying
- (G) the number of hotel rooms needed
- (H) where the family is coming from
- (J) the type of food the family likes to eat

I would like to make dinner reservations at your restaurant for July 3. We would like to be seated by 7:00. Please let me know if you can accommodate us.

3. **Who would be an appropriate person to send this letter to?**
- (A) a relative
- (B) a business owner
- (C) a restaurant manager
- (D) a friend

4. **What needed information is missing from this letter?**
- (F) the number of people who want to eat at the restaurant
- (G) the type of food the people like to eat
- (H) how much money the people plan to spend
- (J) the name of the hotel where the people are staying

 STOP

Name _____ Date_____

LANGUAGE: EXPRESSION
SAMPLE TEST

Directions: Read the directions for each section. Fill in the circle for the answer you think is correct.

> ### Examples
>
> **Find the underlined part that is the simple subject of the sentence.**
>
> A.   The <u>old</u> red <u>barn</u> <u>needed</u> to be <u>painted</u>.
>   Ⓐ   Ⓑ   Ⓒ   Ⓓ
>
> **Find the underlined part that is the simple predicate (verb) of the sentence.**
>
> B.   The <u>lions</u> at the <u>park</u> <u>roared</u> <u>loudly</u>.
>   Ⓕ   Ⓖ   Ⓗ   Ⓙ

For number 1, choose the word or phrase that best completes the sentence.

1. I saw the _____ tree in the world in California.

    Ⓐ tallest
    Ⓑ most tallest
    Ⓒ most taller
    Ⓓ tall

For number 2, choose the answer that is a complete and correctly written sentence.

2.   Ⓕ He didn't hurt hisself when he bumped his head.
     Ⓖ Theys have some concerns about the homework.
     Ⓗ Me and her practiced writing our name backward.
     Ⓙ Rika and I went in-line skating for three hours yesterday.

For numbers 3–5, read each answer choice. Fill in the circle for the choice that has an error. If there are no errors, fill in the fourth circle.

3.   Ⓐ A more better place
     Ⓑ to see bats
     Ⓒ is the Carlsbad Caverns in New Mexico.
     Ⓓ No mistakes

4.   Ⓕ Mom and Aunt Emily
     Ⓖ aren't in no aerobics class
     Ⓗ this Saturday.
     Ⓙ No mistakes

5.   Ⓐ After they finished the books,
     Ⓑ Tom and Larry
     Ⓒ wrote the report.
     Ⓓ No mistakes

For number 6, find the underlined part that is the simple subject of the sentence.

6.   The <u>setting</u> of the <u>play</u> <u>was</u> a <u>castle</u>.
         Ⓕ   Ⓖ Ⓗ   Ⓙ

For number 7, find the underlined part that is the simple predicate (verb) of the sentence.

7.   <u>Heather</u> <u>wants</u> <u>herbs</u> in her <u>garden</u>.
      Ⓐ   Ⓑ   Ⓒ   Ⓓ

GO ON

LANGUAGE: EXPRESSION
SAMPLE TEST (cont.)

For numbers 8–10, choose the answer that best combines the underlined sentences.

8. **Mark will create a collage tomorrow. Mark will use photographs for his collage.**

    (F) Mark will create a collage tomorrow, but he will use photographs.

    (G) Mark will use photographs tomorrow and he will create a collage.

    (H) Mark will create a collage tomorrow and he will use photographs.

    (J) Mark will create a collage tomorrow using photographs.

9. **Amanda took us to the pond. She showed us where to find the ducks on the pond.**

    (A) Amanda showed us where to find the ducks on the pond that she took us to.

    (B) Amanda took us to the pond and showed us where to find the ducks.

    (C) Amanda took us to find the ducks, but also where to find the pond.

    (D) Amanda showed us where to find the pond and also where to find the ducks.

10. **Our town has parks. Our town has beaches. Our town does not have a public swimming pool.**

    (F) Parks and beaches are in our town, but nowhere is there a public swimming pool.

    (G) Our town has parks, beaches, but not a public swimming pool.

    (H) Our town has parks and beaches, but it does not have a public swimming pool.

    (J) A public swimming pool is not in our town, but it does have parks and beaches.

For numbers 11 and 12, choose the best way of expressing the idea.

11. (A) The school yearbook needed photographs, so Jason took photographs of his classmates.

    (B) Jason took photographs of his classmates for the school yearbook.

    (C) Because of the school yearbook, Jason took photographs of his classmates.

    (D) Jason took photographs, for the school yearbook, of his classmates.

12. (F) After we drove to the mountains, we set up our camping gear.

    (G) We were going camping in the mountains, so after the drive, we set up our gear.

    (H) To set up our camping gear, we drove to the mountains.

    (J) Before we set up our camping gear, we drove to the mountains.

GO ON

Name _____   Date_____

LANGUAGE: EXPRESSION
SAMPLE TEST (cont.)

Read the paragraph below. Find the best topic sentence for the paragraph.

_____. Since they were so rare, the sight of early motor cars was exciting to the American public.

13.
- Ⓐ Today's cars are much more varied, comfortable, and fun to drive.
- Ⓑ Taking a car trip was quite a challenge in the early days.
- Ⓒ Not everyone welcomed the first automobiles.
- Ⓓ Gasoline-powered automobiles were available only to a few wealthy individuals before the early 1900s.

Find the answer choice that best develops the topic sentence.

14. **Benjamin Franklin is one of the most important people In American history.**
- Ⓕ His influence has remained with us over 200 years. Today, we see his picture on stamps and on the hundred-dollar bill.
- Ⓖ He died at the age of 84. We still remember him over 200 years later.
- Ⓗ He owned his own printing business and printed a newspaper. He considered printing his career, but he was involved in many other things too.
- Ⓙ He was one of 17 children born in a very poor family in Boston, Massachusetts. He did not receive a very good education.

Read the paragraph below. Find the sentence that does not belong in the paragraph.

(1) Gregory's father worked for the Wildlife Department. (2) One day, he came to Gregory's class carrying a small cage. (3) When Gregory's father left, the students discussed his visit. (4) When he opened the top of the cage, a furry little raccoon popped out.

15.
- Ⓐ Sentence 1
- Ⓑ Sentence 2
- Ⓒ Sentence 3
- Ⓓ Sentence 4

Read the paragraph below. Find the sentence that best fits the blank in the paragraph.

The first comic books were made in 1911. But it wasn't until 1933 that they really became popular. The first best-selling comic books were created by two high school students named Jerry Siegel and Joe Schuster. _____. He performod amazing feats.

16.
- Ⓕ Some people are comic book collectors.
- Ⓖ They wrote their own science fiction magazine about a superhero.
- Ⓗ Nowadays, comic books are created by publishing companies.
- Ⓙ Comic books are sold in stores all over the world.

GO ON

Published by Spectrum. Copyright protected.   978-1-62057-597-0 *Spectrum Test Practice 5*

LANGUAGE: EXPRESSION
SAMPLE TEST (cont.)

Read the story and use it to do numbers 17–20.

(1) Imagine going to a college where you can major in video games! (2) Well, all the students at DigiPen School is doing exactly that. (3) A man named Claude Comair founded the college in Vancouver, British Columbia. (4) It has a goal that is to teach students to create computer animation and to also program video games. (5) While this may sound like fun, the school's curriculum is serious business. (6) The teachers are professional programmers and engineers. (7) The classes are taught year-round for two years of intense study. (8) Students typically from 8 A.M. to 9 P.M. Monday through Friday and for much of the day on Saturday.

17. Which sentence could be added after sentence 6?

- (A) Each game requires several programmers, artists, musicians, and designers to make it marketable.
- (B) The classes include advanced mathematics and physics, computer languages, and art.
- (C) The video game industry earns billions of dollars each year.
- (D) The graduates of DigiPen will tell you that they make a living doing what they love best—playing video games.

18. How is sentence 4 best written?

- (F) Its goal is to teach students to create computer animation and program video games.
- (G) For its goal, it aims to teach students to create computer animation and program video games.
- (H) Creating computer animation and programming video games is the goal the school sets for all of its students.
- (J) Teaching creating computer animation and programming video games is it goal.

19. Which sentence is incomplete?

- (A) Sentence 2
- (B) Sentence 4
- (C) Sentence 6
- (D) Sentence 8

20. In sentence 2, is doing is best written —

- (F) are doing
- (G) was doing
- (H) would be doing
- (J) As it is

STOP

LANGUAGE: SPELLING

● Lesson 18: Spelling Skills

Directions: Follow the directions for each section. Choose the answer you think is correct.

Examples

Find the word that is spelled correctly and fits best in the blank.

A. Elliot _____ a song for the contest.
- (A) composed
- (B) compossed
- (C) compoosed
- (D) compoased

Choose the phrase in which the underlined word is **not** spelled correctly.

B.
- (F) knead the dough
- (G) send a repli
- (H) honor badge
- (J) fiery temper

Clue Be sure you know if you are supposed to find a word that is spelled correctly or incorrectly.

● Practice

For numbers 1–4, find the word that is spelled correctly and fits best in the blank.

1. Samantha had to renew her driver's _____.
   - (A) licensse
   - (B) lisense
   - (C) liesense
   - (D) license

2. Roger certified that the table was a _____ antique.
   - (F) genuwine
   - (G) genuine
   - (H) genuin
   - (J) genuinn

3. Please call a _____ to repair the sink.
   - (A) plumber
   - (B) plummer
   - (C) plumbner
   - (D) plumer

4. Agatha _____ on the her mother's help.
   - (F) relys
   - (G) relies
   - (H) realize
   - (J) reelies

For numbers 5–8, read the phrases. Choose the phrase in which the underlined word is not spelled correctly.

5.
   - (A) free sample
   - (B) mental image
   - (C) a small morsul
   - (D) fried potatoes

6.
   - (F) airtight container
   - (G) horse-driven carriage
   - (H) hopeful fuchure
   - (J) countless stars

7.
   - (A) collapse under pressure
   - (B) elderlie people
   - (C) recite the poem
   - (D) club members were initiated

8.
   - (F) scholarly pursuits
   - (G) sparkling diamonds
   - (H) went down in defeat
   - (J) difficult profesion

STOP

LANGUAGE: SPELLING

● Lesson 19: Spelling Skills

Directions: Follow the directions for each section. Choose the answer you think is correct.

Examples

Fill in the circle for the choice that has a spelling error. If all the words are spelled correctly, fill in the circle for "No mistakes."

A.
- Ⓐ barge
- Ⓑ fasinate
- Ⓒ choir
- Ⓓ No mistakes

Choose the phrase in which the underlined word is not spelled correctly for the way it is used.

B.
- Ⓕ rent is <u>due</u>
- Ⓖ popcorn <u>kernel</u>
- Ⓗ <u>cast</u> party
- Ⓙ <u>beach</u> tree

 Clue If you know which answer is correct, fill in the circle and move on. Do not change your answer unless you are certain that you made a mistake.

● Practice

For numbers 1–3, fill in the circle for the choice that has a spelling error. If there is no mistake, fill in the last answer space.

1.
- Ⓐ kindle
- Ⓑ billiyun
- Ⓒ focus
- Ⓓ No mistakes

2.
- Ⓕ kwaint
- Ⓖ loyal
- Ⓗ pillar
- Ⓙ No mistakes

3.
- Ⓐ pursue
- Ⓑ jealous
- Ⓒ heroic
- Ⓓ No mistakes

For numbers 4–6, read each phrase. One of the underlined words is not spelled correctly for the way it is used in the phrase. Fill in the circle for that phrase.

4.
- Ⓕ worldwide <u>piece</u>
- Ⓖ <u>idle</u> behavior
- Ⓗ wounds will <u>heal</u>
- Ⓙ light the <u>flare</u>

5.
- Ⓐ $50 <u>fare</u>
- Ⓑ lesson <u>learned</u>
- Ⓒ <u>fowl</u> ball
- Ⓓ apple <u>core</u>

6.
- Ⓕ <u>write</u> a message
- Ⓖ <u>herd</u> of buffalo
- Ⓗ results will <u>vary</u>
- Ⓙ tie a <u>not</u>

For numbers 7–9, find the underlined part that is misspelled. If all the words are spelled correctly, fill in the space for "No mistake."

7. I <u>beleive</u> the <u>experiment</u> will prove the
    Ⓐ   Ⓑ
<u>existence</u> of fat in this recipe. <u>No mistake.</u>
    Ⓒ   Ⓓ

8. If you are <u>board</u>, you may go <u>outside</u> and
                    Ⓕ   Ⓖ
rake the <u>leaves</u>. <u>No mistake.</u>
          Ⓗ   Ⓙ

9. Come home <u>strait</u> after school <u>because</u> you
    Ⓐ   Ⓑ   Ⓒ
have an <u>appointment</u>. <u>No mistake.</u>
                            Ⓓ

STOP

Name _____ Date_____

Directions: Follow the directions for each section. Choose the answer you think is correct.

Examples

Find the word that is spelled correctly and fits best in the blank.

A.   An island is _____ by water.

- Ⓐ surownded
- Ⓑ sirrounded
- Ⓒ serrounded
- Ⓓ surrounded

Choose the phrase in which the underlined word is **not** spelled correctly.

B.
- Ⓕ a good <u>impression</u>
- Ⓖ California <u>misions</u>
- Ⓗ prehistoric <u>animals</u>
- Ⓙ torn <u>sleeve</u>

For numbers 1–4, find the word that is spelled correctly and fits best in the blank.

1.   The waiter forgot to give us our _____.

- Ⓐ receipt
- Ⓑ reciept
- Ⓒ recete
- Ⓓ recite

2.   The detective will _____ the crime.

- Ⓕ innvestigate
- Ⓖ envestigate
- Ⓗ investagate
- Ⓙ investigate

3.   The technology _____ is still growing.

- Ⓐ indistry
- Ⓑ industry
- Ⓒ industree
- Ⓓ industri

4.   Shinook addressed the _____ of elders.

- Ⓕ counsill
- Ⓖ cowncil
- Ⓗ council
- Ⓙ counsell

For numbers 5–9, read the phrases. Choose the phrase in which the underlined word is not spelled correctly.

5.
- Ⓐ <u>locked</u> in a <u>dungeon</u>
- Ⓑ <u>casual</u> conversation
- Ⓒ <u>betraid</u> the trust
- Ⓓ <u>introduce</u> your friends

6.
- Ⓕ <u>reckreation</u> area
- Ⓖ <u>knight</u> in <u>shining</u> armor
- Ⓗ <u>hoarse</u> voice
- Ⓙ medium <u>height</u>

7.
- Ⓐ <u>raise</u> sheep
- Ⓑ <u>enough</u> said
- Ⓒ <u>bouquet</u> of balloons
- Ⓓ aunts, uncles, and <u>cusins</u>

8.
- Ⓕ get into <u>trubble</u>
- Ⓖ <u>loose</u> tooth
- Ⓗ stormy <u>weather</u>
- Ⓙ <u>their</u> bikes

9.
- Ⓐ <u>itchy</u> skin
- Ⓑ reduce <u>waste</u>
- Ⓒ <u>bach</u> of cookies
- Ⓓ <u>barge</u> through the door

GO ON

LANGUAGE: SPELLING
SAMPLE TEST (cont.)

For numbers 10–12, read each item. Fill in the circle for the choice that has a spelling error. If there is not mistake, fill in the last answer space.

10. (F) auction
     (G) caught
     (H) autum
     (J) No mistakes

11. (A) grone
     (B) leather
     (C) reason
     (D) No mistakes

12. (F) retreive
     (G) sleigh
     (H) receive
     (J) No mistakes

For numbers 13–15, read each phrase. One of the underlined words is not spelled correctly for the way it is used in the phrase. Fill in the circle for the word that is not spelled correctly.

13. (A) our books
     (B) its raining
     (C) they're in charge
     (D) fined a fee

14. (F) a flair for acting
     (G) minor damage
     (H) plane clothes
     (J) a fishing pier

15. (A) die the fabric
     (B) a broken window pane
     (C) hail, sleet, and snow
     (D) move forth

For numbers 16–19, find the underlined part that is misspelled. If all the words are spelled correctly, fill in the circle for "No mistake."

16. The village residants were wary of the
         (F)   (G)   (H)
     newcomer. No mistake.
                 (J)

17. A worrisome rumor spread threw the
        (A)   (B)   (C)
     school. No mistake.
             (D)

18. He adjusted the bandage to cover the
            (F)   (G)
     blister. No mistake.
        (H)   (J)

19. The evidence proved her guilt. No
         (A)   (B)   (C)
     mistake.
       (D)

STOP

LANGUAGE: STUDY SKILLS

● Lesson 20: Study Skills

Directions: Follow the directions for each section. Fill in the circle for the correct answer.

Example

Baseball

I.   History
   A. Teams
   B. Players
II. Rules
   A. _____
   B. Batting

A. Line II. A. in the outline on the left is blank. Which of these fits best in the blank?

- (A) Umpires
- (B) Coaches
- (C) Pitching
- (D) Mascots

 Clue Think through your answers carefully. Ask yourself if your answer makes sense.

● Practice

The Gold Rush

Table of Contents

Index

1. Look at the table of contents. Which two chapters might tell about how people came to California?
   - (A) Chapters 1 and 2
   - (B) Chapters 2 and 3
   - (C) Chapters 3 and 4
   - (D) Chapters 4 and 5

2. Compare the index to the table of contents. What information do you think the book would provide about Sara Winnemuca?
   - (F) how she came to California
   - (G) what her life was like in the gold mines
   - (H) what her life was like as a child
   - (J) what her life was like after the Gold Rush

3. Look at the table of contents. Which of these might you find in Chapter 1?
   - (A) traveling on a ship
   - (B) traveling in a covered wagon
   - (C) panning for gold
   - (D) schools for the children of gold miners

LANGUAGE: STUDY SKILLS

● Lesson 21: Study Skills

Directions: Follow the directions for each section. Fill in the circle for the answer you think is correct.

Examples

Choose the word that would come first in an alphabetical list.

A.
- Ⓐ Great Britain
- Ⓑ growl
- Ⓒ granola
- Ⓓ grapefruit

Choose the best source of information.

B. **Which of these would help you plan a driving route from Los Angeles to San Francisco?**
- Ⓕ an almanac
- Ⓖ a road atlas
- Ⓗ an encyclopedia
- Ⓙ the owner's manual for an automobile

 Clue Read the directions carefully. Be sure that you know what you are supposed to do for each question.

● Practice

1. **Kim is writing a report on the Liberty Bell. Which of these would Kim not want to include in her report?**
   - Ⓐ a physical description of the Liberty Bell
   - Ⓑ events in which the Liberty Bell has been rung
   - Ⓒ where the Liberty Bell is hung
   - Ⓓ a description of Pennsylvania

2. **In writing her report, Kim used a book titled *Let Liberty Ring*. Where in the book should Kim look to get a general overview of the book's contents?**
   - Ⓕ the title page
   - Ⓖ the introduction
   - Ⓗ the glossary
   - Ⓙ the index

For numbers 3–4, choose the word that would come first in an alphabetical list.

3.
- Ⓐ amber
- Ⓑ amble
- Ⓒ ambassador
- Ⓓ ambulance

4.
- Ⓕ phase
- Ⓖ pharmacy
- Ⓗ pheasant
- Ⓙ phantom

For numbers 5–6, choose the best source of information.

5. **Which of these would tell you another word for *beautiful*?**
   - Ⓐ encyclopedia
   - Ⓑ book of quotations
   - Ⓒ thesaurus
   - Ⓓ almanac

6. **Which of these would help you understand the water cycle?**
   - Ⓕ a map
   - Ⓖ a dictionary
   - Ⓗ a history book
   - Ⓙ an encyclopedia article

 STOP

LANGUAGE: STUDY SKILLS
SAMPLE TEST

Directions: Follow the directions for each section. Fill in the circle for the answer you think is correct.

Examples

A. **What would you find in a table of contents?**

- Ⓐ meanings of words
- Ⓑ chapter titles
- Ⓒ a dedication
- Ⓓ a list of the author's references

B. **Which of these books might provide recipes used in Colonial America?**

- Ⓕ *Building a Log Cabin from Scratch*
- Ⓖ *Native Americans Before Jamestown*
- Ⓗ *Musical Instruments in Early America*
- Ⓙ *A History of Cooking in America*

Study the map below. Use it to answer numbers 1 and 2.

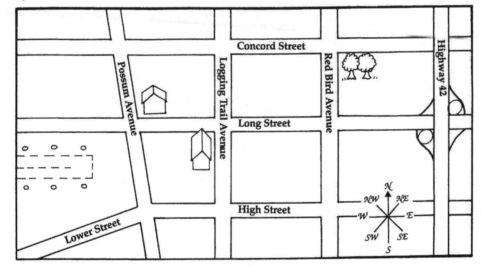

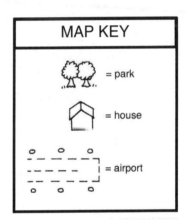

MAP KEY

= park

= house

= airport

1. **Where is the airport located?**

- Ⓐ north of Lower Street and east of High Street
- Ⓑ south of Long Street and west of Possum Avenue
- Ⓒ east of Highway 42 and west of Red Bird Avenue
- Ⓓ south of Concord Street and north of Long Street

2. **If you were to walk from the house at the corner of Long Street and Possum Avenue to the park, which directions would you follow?**

- Ⓕ travel south on Logging Trail Avenue and west on High Street
- Ⓖ travel north on Possum Avenue and west on Long Street
- Ⓗ travel east on Long Street and north on Red Bird Avenue
- Ⓙ travel north on Possum Avenue and west on Concord Street

GO ON

LANGUAGE: STUDY SKILLS
SAMPLE TEST (cont.)

Use the sample dictionary entries and the Pronunciation Guide to answer numbers 3–8.

camp /'kamp/ *n.* 1. a place, usually away from cities, where tents or simple buildings are put up to provide shelter for people working or vacationing there 2. a place, usually in the country, for recreation or instruction during the summer months [goes to summer camp each July] 3. a group of people who work to promote a certain idea or thought or who work together in support of another person *v.* 4. To live temporarily in a camp or outdoors.
cam·paign /kam-'pān/ *n.* 1. A series of military operations that make up a distinct period during a war 2. A series of activities designed to bring about a desired outcome [an election campaign]
v. 3. to conduct a campaign
cam·pus /'kam-pəs/ *n.* 1. The grounds and buildings of a school

Pronunciation Guide:
ash, st**āy**, ə = a in *alone* and u in *circus*, w**e**t, **ē**asy, h**i**t, h**ī**de, f**o**x, g**ō**, b**u**t, m**ū**sic

3. The "u" in campus sounds most like the vowel sound in —
   - (A) but.
   - (B) music.
   - (C) circus.
   - (D) wet.

4. Which definition best fits the word *camp* as it is used in the sentence below?

   The field workers lived in a *camp* a mile away from the farm.
   - (F) 1
   - (G) 2
   - (H) 3
   - (J) 4

5. How many syllables are in the word *campaign*?
   - (A) 1
   - (B) 2
   - (C) 3
   - (D) 4

6. In which of these sentences is *camp* used as a verb?
   - (F) The governor's camp worked through the night to prepare her acceptance speech.
   - (G) Della will go to music camp in July.
   - (H) The hike back to camp took three hours.
   - (J) The family will camp in Yosemite this spring.

7. What part of speech is the word campus?
   - (A) verb
   - (B) noun
   - (C) adjective
   - (D) adverb

8. Look at the words in the sample dictionary. Which guide words would appear on the dictionary page on which these words are located?
   - (F) campground–candle
   - (G) camera–campfire
   - (H) camisole–canal
   - (J) camper–campsite

GO ON

LANGUAGE: STUDY SKILLS
SAMPLE TEST (cont.)

For numbers 9–12, look at the picture of the set of encyclopedias. Each encyclopedia is numbered and contains information about topics that begin with the letters shown on the volume.

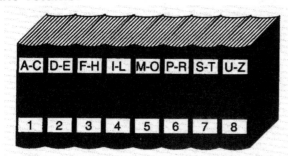

9. Which of these topics would be found in Volume 5?
   - (A) goats
   - (B) nursing
   - (C) a biography of Neil Armstrong
   - (D) the history of Canada

10. In which volume would you find information on dinosaurs?
   - (F) Volume 2
   - (G) Volume 4
   - (H) Volume 6
   - (J) Volume 7

11. Which of these topics would not be found in Volume 1?
   - (A) the game of basketball
   - (B) a biography of Hans Christian Andersen
   - (C) animals
   - (D) a biography of Colin Powell

12. In which volume would you find a map of the United States?
   - (F) Volume 1
   - (G) Volume 3
   - (H) Volume 6
   - (J) Volume 8

Read each question below. Fill in the circle for the answer you think is correct.

13. Look at these guide words from a dictionary page.

   era—everyday

   Which word could be found on the page?
   - (A) evict
   - (B) entire
   - (C) eternal
   - (D) equipment

14. Look at these guide words from a dictionary page.

   license—local

   Which word could be found on the page?
   - (F) locate
   - (G) light
   - (H) liborty
   - (J) logical

15. Which of these is a main heading that includes the other three words?
   - (A) Fruits
   - (B) Grapes
   - (C) Oranges
   - (D) Strawberries

16. Which of these is a main heading that includes the other three words?
   - (F) Oxygen
   - (G) Helium
   - (H) Hydrogen
   - (J) Gases

STOP

LANGUAGE: WRITING

● **Lesson 22: Writing**

Directions: On a separate sheet of paper, write a response to each prompt. Include all the parts in the checklists.

1. **Write an Opinion**

Write a letter to your parent arguing that you should receive a new privilege. It could be staying up later, going someplace on your own, or doing chores for pay.

Checklist:

Read what you wrote. Did you remember to do the following?

	Yes	No
State your opinion.	☐	☐
Include well-organized reasons, facts, examples, and details that support your opinion.	☐	☐
Use words such as *consequently* and *specifically* to link your opinion with reasons.	☐	☐
Write a strong conclusion that summarizes your opinion.	☐	☐

2. **Write an Opinion**

Write a letter to your local newspaper expressing your opinion about something you would like to see changed in your community. It could be a new park or bike path, cleaner streets, or more recreational programs for young people.

Checklist:

Read what you wrote. Did you remember to do the following?

	Yes	No
State your opinion.	☐	☐
Include well-organized reasons, facts, examples, and details that support your opinion.	☐	☐
Use words such as *consequently* and *specifically* to link your opinion with reasons.	☐	☐
Write a strong conclusion that summarizes your opinion.	☐	☐

3. **Write to Inform**

Write an article explaining how people your age can incorporate eating healthy foods into their daily routines. Include ideas about healthy after-school snacks.

Checklist:

Read what you wrote. Did you remember to do the following?

	Yes	No
Introduce the topic clearly.	☐	☐
Include headings, charts, or illustrations if they will help the reader understand.	☐	☐
Include facts, definitions, examples, and details that are organized logically.	☐	☐
Use words such as *in contrast* and *especially* to link ideas.	☐	☐
Write a concluding statement.	☐	☐

GO ON

LANGUAGE: WRITING

● Lesson 22: Writing (cont.)

4. Write to Inform

Write a letter to a younger sibling, cousin, or friend. Explain what he or she will like most about being the age that you are now. Give some advice about how to do well in school, make friends, and keep a good attitude.

Checklist:

Read what you wrote. Did you remember to do the following?

	Yes	No
Introduce the topic clearly.	☐	☐
Include headings, charts, or illustrations if they will help the reader understand.	☐	☐
Include facts, definitions, examples, and details that are organized logically.	☐	☐
Use words such as *in contrast* and *especially* to link ideas.	☐	☐
Write a concluding statement.	☐	☐

5. Write a Narrative

Write a fictional story about your perfect birthday. Where would you go? Who would you see? Begin when you wake up on your birthday, and end when you go to sleep that night.

Checklist:

Read what you wrote. Did you remember to do the following?

	Yes	No
Establish the situation and introduce characters.	☐	☐
Use techniques such as dialogue, description, and pacing to develop the story.	☐	☐
Include words and phrases that show the sequence of events.	☐	☐
Provide sensory details.	☐	☐
Write a good ending.	☐	☐

6. Write a Narrative

Write a story about two characters on a journey to find something in the wilderness or in the city.

Checklist:

Read what you wrote. Did you remember to do the following?

	Yes	No
Establish the situation and introduce characters.	☐	☐
Use techniques such as dialogue, description, and pacing to develop the story.	☐	☐
Include words and phrases that show the sequence of events.	☐	☐
Provide sensory details.	☐	☐
Write a good ending.	☐	☐

STOP

LANGUAGE PRACTICE TEST

● **Part 1: Language Mechanics**

Directions: Fill in the circle next to the punctuation mark that is needed in the sentence. Fill in the space for "None" if no additional punctuation marks are needed.

Example

A. **Many people line the streets to watch the parade**

- (A) !
- (B) .
- (C) ?
- (D) None

1. **Who ate the last meatball?" asked Janet.**

- (A) .
- (B) ,
- (C) "
- (D) None

2. **Mike, Sally and I took a baby-sitting course last summer.**

- (F) ,
- (G) ;
- (H) !
- (J) None

3. **Who's going sledding with me today?**

- (A) "
- (B) ,
- (C) .
- (D) None

4. **On Saturday morning all the neighborhood kids meet to play soccer.**

- (F) :
- (G) .
- (H) ,
- (J) !

For numbers 5–7, fill in the circle next to the choice that has a punctuation error. If there is no mistake, fill in the fourth answer choice.

5.
- (A) Most people
- (B) love pizza but
- (C) he hates it.
- (D) No mistakes

6.
- (F) What do you think
- (G) is in the bag. I think
- (H) it's a cookie.
- (J) No mistakes

7.
- (A) Maria plants flowers and
- (B) raises vegetables
- (C) in her garden.
- (D) No mistakes

For numbers 8 and 9, choose the word or words that fit best in the blank and show the correct punctuation.

8. **On Valentine's Day, _____ class had a party.**

- (F) Miss Jacksons
- (G) Miss Jacksons'
- (H) Miss Jackson's
- (J) Miss Jacksons's

9. **_____ you may carry the water.**

- (A) Yes
- (B) Yes,
- (C) Yes?
- (D) Yes.

GO ON

Name _____   Date_____

For numbers 10–13, read each group of sentences. Fill in the circle next to the sentence that is written correctly and shows the correct capitalization and punctuation.

10. Ⓕ Mrs. Peterson may I check out this book?

    Ⓖ Moms candles come in handy when the power goes out.

    Ⓗ In the morning, dad read us a story.

    Ⓙ Troy and Kenneth sit in the grass and watch the clouds.

11. Ⓐ Ballet dancers create graceful patterns using formal precise movements.

    Ⓑ Last spring, four baby robins hatched.

    Ⓒ Charles Lindbergh was the first person to fly nonstop across the atlantic ocean by himself.

    Ⓓ Suzetto and Jacques speak french at home.

12. Ⓕ A bears home is a den.

    Ⓖ A. A. Milne was born on january 18 1882.

    Ⓗ At our house, green jellybeans are always eaten first.

    Ⓙ Since we don't drive, our mom's are glad to drop us off.

13. Ⓐ Kate helped Alyson and Sara hang up art projects.

    Ⓑ Joels favorite subject is Aviation.

    Ⓒ Maybe I shouldnt have had that second doughnut.

    Ⓓ Kim who left her keys in the car was scolded for her carelessness.

For numbers 14–16, read the sentence with a blank. Fill in the circle for the answer choice that best fits in the blank and has correct punctuation and capitalization.

14. The hospital is on _____ near the park.

    Ⓕ Grant Ave.

    Ⓖ Grant Ave,

    Ⓗ Grant, Ave.

    Ⓙ grant ave.,

15. Many camels live in the _____.

    Ⓐ African And Arabian Deserts

    Ⓑ African And Arabian deserts

    Ⓒ African and Arabian deserts

    Ⓓ african and arabian deserts

16. Every summer I go with my _____ to Camp Muckamucka.

    Ⓕ friends Ben and Mike

    Ⓖ friends, Ben and Mike

    Ⓗ friends Ben and Mike,

    Ⓙ friends, ben and Mike,

Choose the correct answer for number 17.

17. What is the correct way to end a friendly letter?

    Ⓐ Your Friend,

       Jessica

    Ⓑ Your Friend.

       Jessica

    Ⓒ Your friend,

       Jessica

    Ⓓ Your friend

       Jessica

GO ON

═══ LANGUAGE PRACTICE TEST ═══
Part 1: Language Mechanics (cont.)

Brandon is writing an article for his local newspaper about an architect who designed some of the buildings in the Grand Canyon. Read the article and use it to do numbers 18–21.

(1) Mary Elizabeth Jane Colter was one of the few female architects in the United States prior to World War I. **(2)** She graduated from the <u>california school of design</u> and taught art to support her mother and sister. **(3)** <u>In the early 1900s Colter</u> was hired to design and decorate a building for Native American crafts at the Grand Canyon. **(4)** She designed the building in a Hopi pueblo style. **(5)** She wanted her building to look like it had been made long ago, so she used long beams and small branches in the ceiling. **(6)** The building was made from red <u>sandstone ladders</u> connected its uneven rooftops. **(7)** Hopi House, <u>Hermit's Rest</u>, Lookout Studio, Phantom Ranch, Watchtower, and Bright Angel Lodge are six Grand Canyon buildings that were designed by Mary Colter. **(8)** In all of them, Colter created a lived-in look and a feeling of history. **(9)** Four of the buildings are National Historic Landmarks.

18. **In sentence 2, <u>california school of design</u> is best written —**
- (F) California School Of Design
- (G) California School of Design
- (H) California school of design
- (J) As it is

19. **In sentence 3, <u>In the early 1900s Colter</u> is best written —**
- (A) In the early 1900s, Colter
- (B) In the early 1900's Colter,
- (C) In the early, 1900s, Colter
- (D) As it is

20. **In sentence 6, <u>sandstone ladders</u> is best written —**
- (F) sandstone! Ladders
- (G) sandstone, ladder
- (H) sandstone. Ladders
- (J) As it is

21. **In sentence 7, <u>Hermit's Rest</u> is best written —**
- (A) Hermits Rest
- (B) Hermits'es rest
- (C) Hermits's Rest
- (D) As it is

STOP

LANGUAGE PRACTICE TEST

● Part 2: Language Expression

Directions: Read the directions for each section. Fill in the circle for the answer you think is correct.

Example

Find the underlined part that is the simple subject of the sentence.

A.   The <u>camp</u> is <u>located</u> on the northern <u>side</u> of <u>Lake Como</u>.
      Ⓐ   Ⓑ   Ⓒ   Ⓓ

For number 1, choose the word or phrase that best completes the sentence.

1.   **Falling stars _____ the sky above.**

    Ⓐ   was streaked
    Ⓑ   streaking
    Ⓒ   were streaked
    Ⓓ   stroaked

For number 2, choose the answer that is a complete and correctly written sentence.

2.   Ⓕ   I can't never keep my room clean for very long.
    Ⓖ   My grandma has his own way of doing things.
    Ⓗ   Jamie and Scott built a fort in their backyard.
    Ⓙ   Brianna and Kylie went snorkles in the ocean.

For numbers 3–5, fill in the circle for the choice that has a usage error. If there is no mistake, fill in the fourth answer choice.

3.   Ⓐ   The fifth grade class
    Ⓑ   are studying
    Ⓒ   Aesop's fables.
    Ⓓ   No mistakes

4.   Ⓕ   All winter long,
    Ⓖ   the sleeping tulips waited
    Ⓗ   for the warm spring sun.
    Ⓙ   No mistakes

5.   Ⓐ   We seed many
    Ⓑ   beautiful fish and enjoyed
    Ⓒ   the warm ocean water.
    Ⓓ   No mistakes

For number 6, find the underlined part that is the simple subject of the sentence.

6.   <u>My</u> <u>parents</u> <u>speak</u> <u>German</u> and sing
    Ⓕ   Ⓖ   Ⓗ   Ⓙ
German songs.

For number 7, find the underlined part that is the simple predicate (verb) of the sentence.

7.   Every <u>Saturday</u> <u>morning</u>, the club
           Ⓐ   Ⓑ
<u>members</u> <u>meet</u> at the treehouse.
    Ⓒ   Ⓓ

GO ON

LANGUAGE PRACTICE TEST

Part 2: Language Expression (cont.)

For numbers 8–10, choose the answer that best combines the underlined sentences.

8. **Chloe wanted chocolate cake for her birthday party.**
   Chloe wanted vanilla ice cream for her birthday party.

   (F) Chloe wanted chocolate cake but not vanilla ice cream for her birthday party.

   (G) Chloe wanted chocolate cake for her birthday party, and she wanted vanilla ice cream to go with it.

   (H) Chloe wanted chocolate cake and vanilla ice cream for her birthday party.

   (J) Chloe wanted chocolate cake but vanilla ice cream for her birthday party.

9. **Uncle Sid always plants tulip bulbs around the garden.**
   He plants the tulip bulbs in October.

   (A) Uncle Sid plants tulip bulbs in October around the garden.

   (B) Uncle Sid always plants tulip bulbs around the garden in October.

   (C) In October, Uncle Sid around the garden plants the tulip bulbs.

   (D) Uncle Sid always plants tulip bulbs around the garden, and he plants the tulip bulbs in October.

10. **Jeffrey lives around the corner.**
    Jeffrey came over to help me clean the garage.

    (F) He lives around the corner, Jeffrey, who came over to help me clean the garage.

    (G) Jeffrey came over to help me clean the garage, and he lives around the corner.

    (H) Jeffrey, who lives around the corner, who came over to help me clean the garage.

    (J) Jeffrey, who lives around the corner, came over to help me clean the garage.

For numbers 11 and 12, choose the best way of expressing the idea.

11. (A) When I baby-sit, I will play games with the children and read them books.

    (B) To baby-sit, I will play games and read books to children.

    (C) The children will play games and read books when I am there to baby-sit.

    (D) I will play games when I baby-sit and read books.

12. (F) Our vacation was made from a scrapbook of photographs and postcards.

    (G) A scrapbook of photographs and postcards were used for our vacation.

    (H) I used photographs and postcards to make a scrapbook of our vacation.

    (J) Photographs and postcards is what I used to make a scrapbook of our vacation.

GO ON

LANGUAGE PRACTICE TEST
Part 2: Language Expression (cont.)

Read the paragraph below. Find the best topic sentence for the paragraph.

13. _____. Wampum was used to decorate personal items such as clothing, and it was common practice to weave thousands of these beads into wampum belts. The Iroquois exchanged wampum belts as promises to maintain peace and to confirm friendships.

    (A) If a chief was given a wampum belt, it meant he was being invited to come for a visit.

    (B) The Iroquois arranged the beads in designs that had special meaning for keeping records.

    (C) The Keepers of the Wampum were respected people.

    (D) *Wampum* is the name Native Americans gave to white or purple beads made from shells.

Find the answer choice that best develops the topic sentence.

14. **To scientists who study plants, corn is a mystery.**

    (F) It can be eaten in many ways. Some people grind it into flour. Others roast it and eat it whole.

    (G) They know that people in the Americas planted corn as long ago as 4,000 years. But they have not found a wild plant that is the ancestor of corn.

    (H) Ancient people like the Anasazi planted it. They used a sharp stick to make a hole in the soil and then dropped kernels of corn into the hole.

    (J) Look at home or in the grocery store for things that contain corn. Read the labels on packages of food. You'll probably discover that many more things contain corn than you might have guessed!

Read the paragraph below. Find the sentence that does not belong in the paragraph.

15. (1) The Pony Express operated from April 3, 1860, to November 20, 1861. (2) Though it lost money for its owner, it successfully established a 2,000-mile mail route between St. Joseph, Missouri, and Sacramento, California. (3) San Francisco was an important city in California during the 1860s. (4) The mail route was an important way to keep communications open between the North and the West at the beginning of the Civil War.

    (A) Sentence 1

    (B) Sentence 2

    (C) Sentence 3

    (D) Sentence 4

GO ON

LANGUAGE PRACTICE TEST
Part 2: Language Expression (cont.)

Read the article below about an important code that was used during World War II. Use the article to do numbers 16–19.

(1) Many years ago, a young Navajo boy was told that he must not speak his Navajo language in school. (2) Later in his life, he became a United States Marine. (3) As a Marine, he served in World War II. (4) That's when his Navajo language gained new respect from the outside world. (5) He was one of a special group of Navajo code talkers, a communications unit that was sent to islands in the Pacific.

(6) In battle, the code talkers were often among the first to land on beaches. (7) They used their Navajo language to send secret messages by radio to headquarters. (8) For example, in code talk, the Navajo word *tsidi*, which means "bird," stood for aircraft. (9) The code talkers information about the location.

(10) Code talkers could speak both Navajo and English fluently. (11) The code talkers had a dangerous job carrying heavy radios and cables, and the enemy was always on the lookout for them. (12) Some code talkers <u>was awarded</u> medals, such as the Bronze Star, for their bravery and service. (13) The enemy was never able to break the secret code during the war.

16. **How would sentences 2 and 3 best be combined without changing their meaning?**
    - (F) Later in his life, he became a United States Marine and served in World War II.
    - (G) Later in his life, he became a United States Marine, but not in World War II.
    - (H) He became a United States Marine during World War II.
    - (J) In World War II, he became a United States Marine and served the United States.

17. **Which sentence is not a complete thought?**
    - (A) Sentence 1
    - (B) Sentence 4
    - (C) Sentence 9
    - (D) Sentence 13

18. **How is sentence 6 best written?**
    - (F) In battle, and among the first to land on the beaches, were the code talkers.
    - (G) Code talkers, who often were among the first to land on the beaches, were in battle.
    - (H) Landing on beaches first, the code talkers were often in battle.
    - (J) As it is

19. **In sentence 12, <u>was awarded</u> is best written —**
    - (A) were awarded
    - (B) is awarded
    - (C) been awarded
    - (D) have awarded

LANGUAGE PRACTICE TEST

● Part 3: Spelling

Directions: Read the directions for each section. Fill in the circle for the answer you think is correct.

Examples

Fill in the circle for the word that is spelled correctly and fits best in the blank.

A.   We visited a _____ farm.

- (A) dairey
- (B) darey
- (C) dairy
- (D) diary

Choose the phrase in which the underlined word is not spelled correctly.

B.
- (F) befour leaving
- (G) among friends
- (H) in early evening
- (J) come together

For numbers 1–6, fill in the circle for the word that is spelled correctly and fits best in the blank.

1.   The baby's _____ cries awoke everyone in the house.
- (A) schrill
- (B) shrill
- (C) shril
- (D) shriell

2.   The view from the cliffs is _____.
- (F) goregeous
- (G) gorgous
- (H) gorgeous
- (J) gorjus

3.   Pat's grandfather will _____ this spring.
- (A) retire
- (B) retyre
- (C) reetir
- (D) retier

4.   Dina _____ the ball.
- (F) catched
- (G) caut
- (H) cot
- (J) caught

5.   She wore a _____ pair of earrings.
- (A) tinie
- (B) tiny
- (C) tinee
- (D) tynee

6.   The _____ interviewed a celebrity.
- (F) reportur
- (G) reportir
- (H) reproter
- (J) reporter

For numbers 7–10, choose the phrase in which the underlined word is not spelled correctly.

7.
- (A) filtered water
- (B) deep raveene
- (C) lofty goals
- (D) herbal tea

8.
- (F) desparate measures
- (G) fictional story
- (H) expert opinion
- (J) impressive performance

9.
- (A) previously unknown
- (B) musical talent
- (C) bright future
- (D) a well-deserved promoshun

10.
- (F) declare your goals
- (G) make a promise
- (H) profess the truth
- (J) swear an othe

GO ON

LANGUAGE PRACTICE TEST
Part 3: Spelling (cont.)

For numbers 11–13, read each answer. Fill in the circle for the choice that has a spelling error. If there is no mistake, fill in the last answer space.

11.
- (A) emerge
- (B) batery
- (C) disease
- (D) No mistakes

12.
- (F) prosper
- (G) literature
- (H) release
- (J) No mistakes

13.
- (A) tost
- (B) shrink
- (C) sparkle
- (D) No mistakes

For numbers 14–16, read each phrase. One of the underlined words is not spelled correctly for the way it is used in the phrase. Fill in the circle for the word that is not spelled correctly.

14.
- (F) chews activities wisely
- (G) too many projects
- (H) straight hair
- (J) weed the garden

15.
- (A) tow the boat
- (B) turn right
- (C) reel diamond ring
- (D) sweet potatoes

16.
- (F) made by hand
- (G) the mountain's peak
- (H) mist and rain
- (J) a creek on the stairs

For numbers 17–20, find the underlined part that is misspelled. If all words are spelled correctly, fill in the circle for "No mistake."

17. It seems that every year, there are more
(A)
flotes than the year before. No mistake.
(B)   (C)   (D)

18. Niko paints nature scenes especially
(F)   (G)   (H)
well. No mistake.
(J)

19. Camels have broad, bony ridges above
(A)   (B)
each eye to sheild them from the sun.
(C)
No mistake.
(D)

20. The horsess pulled the wagons along the
(F)   (G)
dusty trail. No mistake.
(H)   (J)

STOP

LANGUAGE PRACTICE TEST

● Part 4: Study Skills

Directions: Follow the directions for each section. Fill in the circle for the answer you think is correct.

Example

OUTLINE

Styles of Dance

1. Ballet
2. Swing
3. Jazz
4. _____
5. Hip-Hop

A. **Which of these would fit best in Line 4 of the outline on the left?**
- (A) Classical Approach
- (B) Dancers
- (C) Dance Instruction
- (D) Tap

Study the map below. Use it to do numbers 1 and 2.

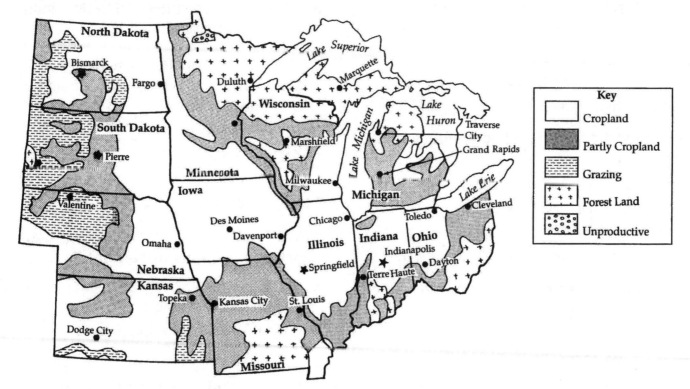

1. **According to the map, most of Iowa's land is used for —**
   - (A) grazing.
   - (B) crops.
   - (C) forests.
   - (D) unproductive uses.

2. **What is the main use for the land around the city of Duluth?**
   - (F) forests
   - (G) grazing
   - (H) unproductive uses
   - (J) crops

GO ON

LANGUAGE PRACTICE TEST
Part 4: Study Skills (cont.)

Use this entry from a library catalog to answer numbers 3–6.

930.67
Cr   **Craft, Brenda**
Lewis and Clark/ Brenda Craft; illustrations
and maps by Drew Allott. Introduction by Marla Singh.
New York: EdBook Publishing Company, 2002.
125 pages; illustrations and maps; 2 cm
(The Explorers series, volume 8)

1. U.S. History   2. Biography   3. Native Americans

---

3. **What is the title of this book?**
   - (A) U.S. History
   - (B) Lewis and Clark
   - (C) Explorers Series
   - (D) Lewis

4. **How did Drew Allott contribute to this book?**
   - (F) He was the illustrator.
   - (G) He was the author.
   - (H) He wrote the introduction.
   - (J) He was the publisher.

5. **In what year was this book published?**
   - (A) 1999
   - (B) 2000
   - (C) 2001
   - (D) 2002

6. **How did Brenda Craft contribute to this book?**
   - (F) She was the publisher.
   - (G) She was the illustrator.
   - (H) She was the author.
   - (J) She wrote a review for it.

Read each question below. Fill in the circle for the correct answer.

7. **Look at these guide words from a dictionary page. Which word would be found on this page?**

   | reason—reduce |

   - (A) realize
   - (B) reign
   - (C) refer
   - (D) receive

8. **Which of these is a main heading that includes the other three words?**
   - (F) Baseball
   - (G) Track and Field
   - (H) Summer Olympic Events
   - (J) Gymnastics

9. **Which of these might be found in a book chapter entitled "Community Service Careers"?**
   - (A) architect
   - (B) firefighter
   - (C) engineer
   - (D) stockbroker

STOP

MATH: CONCEPTS

● Lesson 1: Numeration

Directions: Read each problem. Fill in the circle for the correct answer.

Examples

A. Which two numbers are both factors of 63?

- (A) 6, 10
- (B) 6, 12
- (C) 7, 8
- (D) 7, 9

B. Which of these is between 2.07 and 2.75 in value?

- (F) 2.03
- (G) 2.70
- (H) 27.0
- (J) 2.85

 Clue Use scratch paper to work the problems. Drawing pictures can help you find the answers to many problems.

● Practice

1. 25 =

- (A) 10^3
- (B) 12^2
- (C) 5^5
- (D) 5^2

2. Which point on this number line shows 654?

- (F) A
- (G) B
- (H) C
- (J) D

3. Which of these will have a remainder when it is divided by 8?

- (A) 40
- (B) 45
- (C) 24
- (D) 56

4. What number is expressed by

$$(9 \times 1{,}000) + (4 \times 100) + (2 \times 10) + (3 \times 1)\ ?$$

- (F) 9,420
- (G) 9,400
- (H) 90,423
- (J) 9,423

5. Maria is fourteenth in line to buy a movie ticket. Exactly how many people are in front of her in line?

- (A) 13
- (B) 15
- (C) 14
- (D) 12

STOP

MATH: CONCEPTS

● Lesson 2: Numeration

Directions: Read each problem. Fill in the circle for the correct answer.

Examples

A. $\sqrt{36} =$

- Ⓐ 6
- Ⓑ 9
- Ⓒ 4
- Ⓓ 13

B. Which of these is the expanded numeral for 1,123?

- Ⓕ 1,000 + 12 + 3
- Ⓖ 11 + 23
- Ⓗ 10,000 + 1,000 + 23
- Ⓙ 1,000 + 100 + 20 + 3

 Clue Read the problems carefully. If you misread a number, it could cause you to make a mistake.

● Practice

1. Which of these numbers cannot be evenly divided into 28?

- Ⓐ 1
- Ⓑ 4
- Ⓒ 6
- Ⓓ 7

2. A librarian was putting books on shelves. There were 58 books and 6 shelves. The librarian wanted to put the same number of books on each shelf, but she had some extras. How many books did <u>not</u> fit on the 6 shelves?

- Ⓕ 4
- Ⓖ 6
- Ⓗ 8
- Ⓙ 9

3. What is the meaning of 640?

- Ⓐ 6 tens and 4 ones
- Ⓑ 6 tens and 0 ones
- Ⓒ 4 hundreds and 6 ones
- Ⓓ 6 hundreds and 4 tens

4. Which of these is <u>not</u> another way to write the number 4,860?

- Ⓕ 400 + 800 + 6 + 0
- Ⓖ four thousand, eight hundred, sixty
- Ⓗ 4,000 + 800 + 60
- Ⓙ

thousands	hundreds	tens	ones
4	8	6	0

5. How many of these numbers are common multiples of 3 and 9?

| 18 | 27 | 58 | 63 | 144 |

- Ⓐ 2
- Ⓑ 3
- Ⓒ 4
- Ⓓ 5

6. What is the smallest number that can be divided evenly by 6 and 15?

- Ⓕ 24
- Ⓖ 30
- Ⓗ 45
- Ⓙ 60

STOP

MATH: CONCEPTS

● Lesson 3: Number Concepts

Directions: Read each problem. Fill in the circle for the correct answer.

Examples

A. Which of these has a 4 in the hundreds place?

(A) 4,523

(B) 8,634

(C) 3,844

(D) 7,498

B. Which of these is an even number?

(F) 34

(G) 57

(H) 21

(J) 19

 Clue Look for key words, numbers, and patterns to help you find the answers.

● Practice

1. What is another name for the Roman numeral XII?

(A) 5

(B) 7

(C) 12

(D) 20

2. What is the rule shown by the number sequence in the box?

3, 5, 7, 9, 11

(F) $n \div 2$

(G) $n \times 2$

(H) $n - 2$

(J) $n + 2$

3. 795,643 =

(A) seven hundred million, ninety-five thousand, six hundred forty-three

(B) seven hundred ninety-five thousand, six hundred forty-three

(C) seven hundred ninety-five million, six thousand forty-three

(D) seven hundred ninety-five, six hundred forty-three

4. Which statement about place value is true?

(F) 10 thousands are equal to 1,000,000

(G) 10 hundreds are equal to 10,000

(H) 10 tens are equal to 1,000

(J) 10 tens are equal to 100

5. Which of these statements is true about the numbers in the box?

4, 9, 16, 25, 36

(A) They are all even numbers.

(B) They are all odd numbers.

(C) They are all perfect squares.

(D) They are all prime numbers.

STOP

MATH: CONCEPTS

● **Lesson 4: Number Concepts**

Directions: Read each problem. Fill in the circle for the correct answer.

Examples

A. Which of these numbers is both odd and a multiple of 5?

- (A) 37
- (B) 25
- (C) 60
- (D) 42

B. In which of these numerals does 7 have the least value?

- (F) 7,302
- (G) 4,675
- (H) 1,257
- (J) 2,796

 Clue Look carefully at the position of the digits within each numeral. The position tells you what value the number has.

● **Practice**

1. These squares show groups of numbers that are related by the same rule. What number is missing from the third square?

128	32
16	4

192	48
24	6

96	?
12	3

- (A) 12
- (B) 36
- (C) 24
- (D) 48

2. How much would the value of 42,369 be increased by replacing the 3 with a 5?

- (F) 200
- (G) 300
- (H) 400
- (J) 500

3. What does the 6 in 678,009 mean?

- (A) 6,000
- (B) 600
- (C) 600,000
- (D) 60,000

4. Suppose you have the digits 1, 5, and 9. Without repeating a digit, how many three-digit numbers could you make with 9 as the ones digit?

- (F) 2
- (G) 3
- (H) 4
- (J) 5

5. Which of these is 6,809,465?

- (A) six billion, eight hundred million, nine thousand, four hundred sixty-five
- (B) six million, eight hundred nine, four hundred sixty-five
- (C) sixty-eight thousand, nine thousand, four hundred sixty-five
- (D) six million, eight hundred nine thousand, four hundred sixty-five

6. Which is the numeral for four million, six hundred ninety-three thousand, three hundred twenty-one?

- (F) 400,693,321
- (G) 4,693,321
- (H) 469,321
- (J) 4,963,231

STOP

MATH: CONCEPTS

● Lesson 5: Properties

Directions: Read each problem. Fill in the circle for the correct answer.

Examples

A. What is 654,909 rounded to the nearest thousand?

- (A) 654,000
- (B) 650,000
- (C) 654,900
- (D) 655,000

B. What is another name for 4 x (2 + 3)?

- (F) 4 x (3 + 2)
- (G) (4 x 2) + 3
- (H) (2 + 3) ÷ 4
- (J) 4 x (2 x 3)

 Clue Some problems can be solved through estimation. When estimating, it is especially important to look for key words and numbers to help you solve the problem.

● Practice

1. There are 324 students in the fifth grade. Each student pledged to read 50 books during the year. Which number sentence shows how to find the number of books the fifth graders pledged to read?

- (A) 324 ÷ 50 = □
- (B) 324 x 50 = □
- (C) 324 + 50 = □
- (D) 324 − 50 = □

2. Which number sentence below is incorrect?

- (F) 4 x 12 = 48
- (G) 0 ÷ 12 = 12
- (H) 4 + 12 = 16
- (J) 48 − 12 = 36

3. What number makes all the number sentences below true?

3 x □ = 15
□ x 6 = 30
9 x □ = 45

- (A) 3
- (D) 6
- (C) 4
- (D) 5

4. The sum of 631 and 892 is closest to —

- (F) 1,600
- (G) 1,500
- (H) 1,300
- (J) 1,400

5. Another name for 20 x 10,000 is —

- (A) 2 x 200,000
- (B) 20,000 x 100
- (C) 200 x 1,000
- (D) 2,000 x 1,000

STOP

MATH: CONCEPTS

● **Lesson 6: Properties**

Directions: Read each problem. Fill in the circle for the correct answer.

Examples

A. What should replace the circle below to make the number sentence true?

$$18 + 5 \bigcirc 5 \times 5$$

- (A) >
- (B) <
- (C) =
- (D) ≥

B. Which statement is true about the answer to the equation in the box?

$$8,986 \div 100 = \square$$

- (F) is between 87 and 88
- (G) is between 88 and 89
- (H) is between 89 and 90
- (J) is between 90 and 91

 Clue Think about which operation is needed to solve an equation—addition, subtraction, multiplication, or division.

● **Practice**

1. Which of these is the best estimate of 66 x 98?
   - (A) 60 x 90
   - (B) 70 x 90
   - (C) 60 x 100
   - (D) 70 x 100

2. What symbol should replace the box in the number sentence below?

   $$64 \; \square \; 8 = 32 \div 4$$

   - (F) x
   - (G) ÷
   - (H) −
   - (J) +

3. The amounts below show how much a student earned during a six-week time period.

$41.87	$36.23
$25.90	$42.36
$34.21	$27.83

   What operations are necessary to find out the student's average weekly earnings?
   - (A) subtraction and addition
   - (B) addition and multiplication
   - (C) addition and division
   - (D) multiplication and division

4. Which of the following number facts does not belong to the same family or group as the number sentence in the box?

   $$6 \times 8 = 48$$

   - (F) 48 ÷ 6 = 8
   - (G) 8 x 6 = 48
   - (H) 48 ÷ 8 = 6
   - (J) 48 ÷ 12 = 4

STOP

MATH: CONCEPTS

● Lesson 7: Place Value

Directions: Choose the best answer for each question.

Examples

A. What is 3.4256 rounded to the nearest hundredth?

- Ⓐ 3.4
- Ⓑ 3.426
- Ⓒ 3
- Ⓓ 3.43

B. How does the product of 7×10^4 relate to 7?

- Ⓕ It has 4 zeros added to 7.
- Ⓖ It has 3 zeros added to 7.
- Ⓗ It has a decimal with 4 zeros before 7.
- Ⓙ It has a decimal with 3 zeros before 7.

● Practice

1. Which shows 2.54 in expanded form?

- Ⓐ $2 \times 100 + 5 \times 10 + 4 \times 1$
- Ⓑ $2 \times 1 + 5 \times (\frac{1}{100}) + 4 \times (\frac{1}{1000})$
- Ⓒ $2 \times (\frac{1}{10}) + 5 \times (\frac{1}{100}) + 4 \times (\frac{1}{1000})$
- Ⓓ $2 \times 1 + 5 \times (\frac{1}{10}) + 4 \times (\frac{1}{100})$

2. Which is true?

- Ⓕ 0.972 = 0.927
- Ⓖ 0.386 < 0.391
- Ⓗ 0.587 > 0.589
- Ⓙ 0.17 > 0.176

3. How does the quotient $6,000,000 \div 10^5$ relate to 6,000,000?

- Ⓐ It has 4 fewer zeros at the end of the number.
- Ⓑ It has 5 fewer zeros at the end of the number.
- Ⓒ It has 4 more zeros at the end of the number.
- Ⓓ It has 5 more zeros at the end of the number.

4. How does the product of 0.359×10^3 relate to 0.359?

- Ⓕ It has the same digits, but the decimal moves 2 places right.
- Ⓖ It has the same digits, but the decimal moves 3 places right.
- Ⓗ It has the same digits, but the decimal moves 2 places left.
- Ⓙ It has the same digits, but the decimal moves 3 places left.

5. What is 19.578 rounded to the nearest tenth?

- Ⓐ 20
- Ⓑ 19.6
- Ⓒ 19.58
- Ⓓ 19.57

6. What is 0.8996 rounded to the nearest thousandth?

- Ⓕ 0.9
- Ⓖ 0.899
- Ⓗ 0.89
- Ⓙ 1

STOP

━━━━━ MATH: CONCEPTS ━━━━━

● Lesson 8: Fractions and Decimals

Directions: Read each problem. Fill in the circle for the correct answer.

Examples

A. Which figure below is $\frac{4}{9}$ shaded?

Ⓐ Ⓑ Ⓒ Ⓓ

B. Which group of decimals is ordered from least to greatest?

Ⓕ 4.482, 4.483, 4.481, 4.408

Ⓖ 4.576, 4.432, 4.678, 4.104

Ⓗ 4.978, 4.652, 4.331, 4.320

Ⓙ 4.269, 4.692, 4.699, 4.732

Clue If you work on scratch paper, be sure that you transfer your answer correctly. Fill in the right answer space.

● Practice

1. Which fraction is shown by the X on this number line?

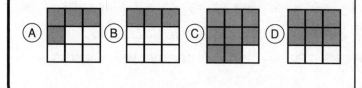

Ⓐ $\frac{3}{5}$

Ⓑ $\frac{1}{3}$

Ⓒ $\frac{7}{15}$

Ⓓ $\frac{5}{10}$

2. The length of YZ is what fraction of the length of VX?

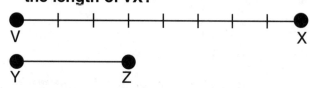

Ⓕ $\frac{7}{12}$

Ⓖ $\frac{5}{10}$

Ⓗ $\frac{4}{8}$

Ⓙ $\frac{3}{8}$

3. Which of these is another way to write $\frac{3}{10}$?

Ⓐ 0.03

Ⓑ 0.3

Ⓒ 3.0

Ⓓ 0.003

4. How do you write thirty-eight hundredths as a decimal?

Ⓕ 03.8

Ⓖ 0.038

Ⓗ 0.38

Ⓙ 3.8

STOP

—————————————— **MATH: CONCEPTS** ——————————————

● Lesson 9: Fractions and Decimals

Directions: Read each problem. Fill in the circle for the correct answer.

Example

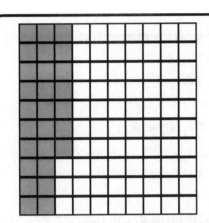

A. **Which decimal shows how much of the shape on the left is shaded?**

- Ⓐ 0.23
- Ⓑ 0.27
- Ⓒ 0.49
- Ⓓ 0.72

Clue Remember that with fractions, the smaller the denominator, the larger the value. The denominator is the numeral on the bottom of the fraction.

● Practice

1. $\frac{3}{\square} = \frac{9}{21}$

   $\square = ?$

   - Ⓐ 8
   - Ⓑ 4
   - Ⓒ 6
   - Ⓓ 7

2. **Which number tells how much of this group of shapes is shaded?**

   - Ⓕ $\frac{3}{4}$
   - Ⓖ $3\frac{1}{2}$
   - Ⓗ $3\frac{1}{4}$
   - Ⓙ $3\frac{3}{4}$

3. **Which of these is another way to write 0.25?**

   - Ⓐ $\frac{1}{4}$
   - Ⓑ $\frac{25}{50}$
   - Ⓒ $\frac{4}{25}$
   - Ⓓ $\frac{3}{8}$

4. **Which of these has a value greater than $\frac{3}{4}$?**

   - Ⓕ 0.25
   - Ⓖ 0.68
   - Ⓗ 0.86
   - Ⓙ 0.75

5. **What is the least common denominator of $\frac{1}{2}$, $\frac{1}{4}$, and $\frac{1}{5}$?**

   - Ⓐ 15
   - Ⓑ 20
   - Ⓒ 30
   - Ⓓ 40

STOP

MATH: CONCEPTS

● **Lesson 10: Patterns, Expressions, Ordered Pairs**

Directions: Choose the best answer for each question.

Examples

A. Which expression matches the statement *three more than the product of five and six*?

- Ⓐ $3 + 5 \times 6$
- Ⓑ $(3 + 5) \times 6$
- Ⓒ $3 \times (5 + 6)$
- Ⓓ $5 \times (3 + 6)$

B. Which is not true about the patterns?
3, 5, 7, 9, 11, . . .
4, 6, 8, 10, 12, . . .

- Ⓕ Both patterns are increasing.
- Ⓖ Both patterns use the rule *add 2*.
- Ⓗ Each term in the second pattern is two times a term in the first pattern.
- Ⓙ Each term in the second pattern is 1 greater than a term in the first pattern.

● **Practice**

1. Which is true about the points on the graph?

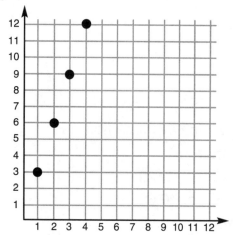

- Ⓐ Add 2 to the *y* value to get the *x* value.
- Ⓑ Add 2 to the *x* value to get the *y* value.
- Ⓒ Multiply the *y* value by 3 to get the *x* value.
- Ⓓ Multiply the *x* value by 3 to get the *y* value.

2. Which expression matches the statement *subtract 4 from 11, then multiply by 8*?

- Ⓕ $(4 - 11) \times 8$
- Ⓖ $(4 - 11) + 8$
- Ⓗ $(11 - 4) \times 8$
- Ⓙ $(11 - 4) + 8$

3. Which set of points matches the rules? *Add 2 to the previous x value. Add 5 to the previous y value.*

- Ⓐ (1, 3), (6, 5), (11, 7), (16, 9), (21, 11)
- Ⓑ (1, 3), (3, 8), (5, 13), (7, 18), (9, 23)
- Ⓒ (1, 3), (2, 15), (4, 75), (8, 375), (16, 1,875)
- Ⓓ (1, 3), (5, 6), (25, 12), (125, 24), (625, 48)

MATH: CONCEPTS
SAMPLE TEST

Directions: Read each problem. Fill in the circle for the correct answer.

Examples

A. What is the value of *n* in the number sentence 6 x *n* = 30?

(A) 4
(B) 5
(C) 6
(D) 7

B. $2\frac{33}{100} =$

(F) 23.3
(G) 0.233
(H) 233
(J) 2.33

---

1. What is the value of 6 in 89.634?

(A) 6 tens
(B) 6 hundreds
(C) 6 tenths
(D) 6 hundredths

2. Which of these is the same as the number in the place value chart?

thousands	hundreds	tens	ones
1	3	8	0

(F) 4,830
(G) four thousand, thirty-eight
(H) 4,000 + 380 + 80
(J) 4,380

3. What number makes these number sentences true?

9 + □ = 15
42 ÷ 7 = □

(A) 6
(B) 4
(C) 12
(D) 9

4. Suppose you wanted to triple the value of 7 and then subtract 15 from it. Which number sentence would you use?

(F) 15 – 73
(G) (7 x 7 x 7) – 15
(H) (7 x 3) – 15
(J) 7 + 7 + 7 + 15

5. What decimal goes in the box on the number line below?

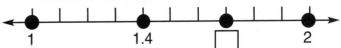

(A) 1.5
(B) 1.6
(C) 1.7
(D) 1.8

6. Which of these is a prime number?

(F) 19
(G) 21
(H) 32
(J) 48

7. What are all of the factors of the product 5 x 4?

(A) 2, 4, 5, and 10
(B) 1, 2, 4, 5, 10, and 20
(C) 1, 4, 5, and 9
(D) 1, 2, 3, 4, 5, 6, 10, and 20

GO ON

Read each problem. Fill in the circle for the correct answer.

8. **Which of these is between 673,904 and 678,042?**

   (F) 675,864

   (G) 673,901

   (H) 672,075

   (J) 678,069

9. **Which of these is another name for $\frac{7}{11}$?**

   (A) $\frac{21}{35}$

   (B) $\frac{35}{66}$

   (C) $\frac{28}{44}$

   (D) $\frac{11}{15}$

10. **If the pattern of the shaded blocks was continued, how many would be shaded in the last figure?**

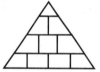

   (F) 0

   (G) 6

   (H) 8

   (J) 10

11. **What number is 1,000 more than 4,568?**

   (A) 3,568

   (B) 5,648

   (C) 5,568

   (D) 4,668

12. **Which of these numbers is 10 less than the Roman numeral XXV?**

   (F) 10

   (G) 17

   (H) 15

   (J) 25

13. **Which is another name for 36 x 1,000?**

   (A) 360 x 100

   (B) 360 x 1,000

   (C) 36 x 100

   (D) 360 x 10,000

14. **In which numeral is there a 3 in both the hundreds and the hundred thousands place?**

   (F) 3,409,397

   (G) 1,306,322

   (H) 2,343,178

   (J) 2,430,390

15. **Which of these rules is not correct?**

   (A) $a \times b = b \div a$

   (B) $a + b = b + a$

   (C) if $a - b = c$, then $c + b = a$

   (D) $(a \times b) + c = (b \times a) + c$

16. **Which number shows the value of the shaded portion of this figure?**

   (F) 0.8

   (G) 0.6

   (H) 0.5

   (J) 2.1

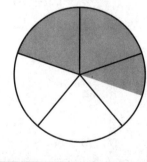

STOP

MATH: COMPUTATION

● Lesson 11: Addition and Subtraction of Whole Numbers

Directions: Solve each problem. Fill in the circle for the correct answer. Choose "None of these" if the correct answer is not given.

Examples

38 + 15		2,554 − 9	

A.
- (A) 23
- (B) 53
- (C) 413
- (D) None of these

B.
- (F) 2,553
- (G) 2,555
- (H) 2,543
- (J) None of these

 Clue Use scratch paper to work out the problems.

● Practice

1. 30 + 15 + 27 =
- (A) 62
- (B) 78
- (C) 72
- (D) None of these

5. 68 − 9 =
- (A) 59
- (B) 61
- (C) 58
- (D) None of these

2. 56 + 47 + 4 =
- (F) 107
- (G) 93
- (H) 110
- (J) None of these

6. 74 − 6 =
- (F) 65
- (G) 09
- (H) 80
- (J) None of these

3.
```
   375
   246
 + 381
```
- (A) 902
- (B) 1,002
- (C) 1,200
- (D) None of these

7.
```
  9,003
− 7,685
```
- (A) 1,428
- (B) 1,328
- (C) 1,318
- (D) None of these

4.
```
  4,553
  8,120
  2,697
+ 1,453
```
- (F) 16,123
- (G) 14,144
- (H) 16,023
- (J) None of these

8.
```
 18,312
− 9,264
```
- (F) 9,048
- (G) 9,124
- (H) 9,158
- (J) None of these

STOP

MATH: COMPUTATION

● Lesson 12: Multiplication and Division of Whole Numbers

Directions: Solve each problem. Fill in the circle for the correct answer. Choose "None of these" if the correct answer is not given.

Examples

A. 42 x 2 =
- (A) 64
- (B) 48
- (C) 84
- (D) None of these

B. 768 ÷ 3 =
- (F) 256
- (G) 323
- (H) 222
- (J) None of these

 Clue Look at all the answer choices before selecting the one you think is correct.

● Practice

1. 801 x 7 =
- (A) 1,507
- (B) 5,607
- (C) 567
- (D) None of these

2. 27
x 36
- (F) 972
- (G) 729
- (H) 613
- (J) None of these

3. 312
x 32
- (A) 6,034
- (B) 1,560
- (C) 9,986
- (D) None of these

4. 8 x 4 x 5 =
- (F) 100
- (G) 160
- (H) 140
- (J) None of these

5. 780 ÷ 12 =
- (A) 65
- (B) 82
- (C) 73
- (D) None of these

6. 23)1,334
- (F) 47
- (G) 63 R4
- (H) 58
- (J) None of these

7. 4)854
- (A) 213 R2
- (B) 211 R3
- (C) 215 R1
- (D) None of these

8. 798 ÷ 6 =
- (F) 123 R1
- (G) 111 R3
- (H) 133
- (J) None of these

STOP

MATH: COMPUTATION

● Lesson 13: Adding Fractions

Directions: Solve each problem. Reduce the answer to its lowest terms. Fill in the circle for the correct answer. Choose "None of these" if the correct answer is not given.

Example

A.

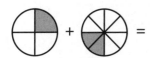 + =

Ⓐ   Ⓒ

Ⓑ   Ⓓ None of these

 Clue After you add the fractions, reduce the answer to its lowest terms.

● Practice

1. $\frac{6}{18} + \frac{2}{18} =$

Ⓐ $\frac{8}{36}$

Ⓓ $\frac{12}{18}$

Ⓒ $\frac{4}{9}$

Ⓓ None of these

4. $\frac{2}{8} + \frac{3}{4} =$

Ⓕ $\frac{5}{12}$

Ⓖ $\frac{5}{8}$

Ⓗ $\frac{3}{16}$

Ⓙ None of these

2. $\frac{3}{13} + \frac{7}{13} =$

Ⓕ $\frac{4}{13}$

Ⓖ $\frac{10}{13}$

Ⓗ $\frac{10}{26}$

Ⓙ None of these

5. $1\frac{5}{9} + 4\frac{3}{9} =$

Ⓐ $5\frac{8}{9}$

Ⓑ $5\frac{2}{9}$

Ⓒ $2\frac{4}{9}$

Ⓓ None of these

3. $\frac{3}{4} + \frac{1}{5} =$

Ⓐ $\frac{1}{5}$

Ⓑ $\frac{4}{9}$

Ⓒ $\frac{19}{20}$

Ⓓ None of these

6. $2\frac{4}{7} + 2\frac{3}{7} =$

Ⓕ 6

Ⓖ $4\frac{6}{7}$

Ⓗ 5

Ⓙ None of these

STOP

MATH: COMPUTATION

● Lesson 14: Subtracting Fractions

Directions: Solve each problem. Reduce the answer to its lowest terms. Fill in the circle for the correct answer. Choose "None of these" if the correct answer is not given.

Examples

A. $\frac{5}{6} - \frac{2}{6} =$

- Ⓐ $\frac{2}{6}$
- Ⓑ $\frac{1}{2}$
- Ⓒ $\frac{4}{6}$
- Ⓓ None of these

B.
$$4$$
$$-2\frac{1}{2}$$

- Ⓕ $1\frac{1}{2}$
- Ⓖ $2\frac{1}{2}$
- Ⓗ $1\frac{3}{4}$
- Ⓙ None of these

 Clue When reducing fractions, be sure to divide the numerator and the denominator by the same number.

● Practice

1. $\frac{8}{15} - \frac{2}{15} =$

- Ⓐ $\frac{2}{5}$
- Ⓑ $\frac{6}{15}$
- Ⓒ $\frac{3}{5}$
- Ⓓ None of these

4.
$$\frac{3}{5}$$
$$-\frac{4}{15}$$

- Ⓕ $\frac{1}{3}$
- Ⓖ $\frac{13}{15}$
- Ⓗ $\frac{8}{15}$
- Ⓙ None of these

2.
$$\frac{6}{7}$$
$$-\frac{3}{7}$$

- Ⓕ $\frac{4}{7}$
- Ⓖ 3
- Ⓗ $\frac{9}{7}$
- Ⓙ None of these

5. $6\frac{3}{8} - 5\frac{5}{8} =$

- Ⓐ $\frac{3}{8}$
- Ⓑ $\frac{3}{4}$
- Ⓒ $1\frac{1}{4}$
- Ⓓ None of these

3. $\frac{4}{5} - \frac{1}{6} =$

- Ⓐ $\frac{1}{10}$
- Ⓑ $\frac{29}{30}$
- Ⓒ $\frac{19}{30}$
- Ⓓ None of these

6.
$$11\frac{12}{15}$$
$$-5\frac{8}{15}$$

- Ⓕ $6\frac{1}{3}$
- Ⓖ $5\frac{4}{15}$
- Ⓗ $6\frac{3}{15}$
- Ⓙ None of these

STOP

MATH: COMPUTATION

● Lesson 15: Multiplying and Dividing Fractions

Directions: Choose the best answer for each question.

Examples

A. $\frac{3}{4} \times \frac{2}{3} = \square$

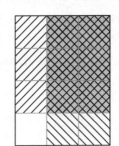

- (A) $\frac{1}{2}$
- (B) $\frac{17}{12}$
- (C) $\frac{11}{12}$
- (D) $\frac{5}{6}$

B. $3 \div \frac{1}{6} = \square$

- (F) 12
- (G) 15
- (H) 18
- (J) 24

● Practice

1. Marta is making a cake recipe that calls for $1\frac{1}{2}$ cups of walnuts. She wants her cake to be 3 times the size of what the recipe would normally make. How many cups of walnuts should Marta use?

   - (A) $3\frac{1}{2}$ cups
   - (B) 4 cups
   - (C) $4\frac{1}{2}$ cups
   - (D) 3 cups

2. Multiplying $\frac{5}{8}$ by which fraction will result in a product greater than $\frac{5}{8}$?

   - (F) $\frac{3}{4}$
   - (G) $\frac{6}{6}$
   - (H) $\frac{8}{9}$
   - (J) $\frac{7}{5}$

3. If 6 people want to share a 25-pound box of vegetables, how many pounds of vegetables should each person get?

   - (A) $\frac{6}{25}$ pound
   - (B) $4\frac{1}{6}$ pounds
   - (C) $\frac{1}{6}$ pound
   - (D) $\frac{1}{25}$ pound

4. What is the area of the rectangle?

   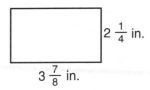

   $2\frac{1}{4}$ in.

   $3\frac{7}{8}$ in.

   - (F) $6\frac{1}{8}$ square inches
   - (G) $6\frac{7}{32}$ square inches
   - (H) $8\frac{1}{8}$ square inches
   - (J) $8\frac{23}{32}$ square inches

GO ON

 978-1-62057-597-0 *Spectrum Test Practice 5*

MATH: COMPUTATION

● Lesson 15: Multiplying and Dividing Fractions (cont.)

5. Harry had $\frac{1}{3}$ of a sub sandwich left over. He cut the leftover sub into 4 equal pieces. What fraction of the original sub was each piece?

    Ⓐ $\frac{1}{4}$

    Ⓑ $\frac{1}{12}$

    Ⓒ $\frac{1}{7}$

    Ⓓ $\frac{1}{8}$

6. $\frac{8}{9} \div 4 = \square$

    Ⓕ $\frac{2}{9}$

    Ⓖ $\frac{1}{9}$

    Ⓗ $\frac{8}{13}$

    Ⓙ $3\frac{5}{9}$

7. A container of 53 strawberries will be shared equally by 4 people. Between what two whole numbers is the amount each person will get?

    Ⓐ 10 and 11

    Ⓑ 11 and 12

    Ⓒ 12 and 13

    Ⓓ 13 and 14

8. Of Karl's T-shirts, $\frac{3}{4}$ are white. Of those, $\frac{2}{5}$ have a design on the front. What fraction of Karl's total T-shirt collection is white with a design on the front?

    Ⓕ $\frac{7}{20}$

    Ⓖ $\frac{3}{10}$

    Ⓗ $\frac{5}{9}$

    Ⓙ $\frac{8}{15}$

9. $\frac{9}{10} \div 12 = \square$?

    Ⓐ $\frac{3}{40}$

    Ⓑ $10\frac{4}{5}$

    Ⓒ $\frac{1}{10}$

    Ⓓ $\frac{4}{30}$

10. $15 \div \frac{7}{12} = \square$

    Ⓕ $18\frac{3}{4}$

    Ⓖ $8\frac{3}{4}$

    Ⓗ $25\frac{5}{7}$

    Ⓙ $21\frac{5}{7}$

11. A recipe calls for 2 cups of flour. The only measuring cup Tracy can find is $\frac{1}{4}$ cup. How many times must Tracy fill this cup to have enough flour?

    Ⓐ 2

    Ⓑ 4

    Ⓒ 6

    Ⓓ 8

GO ON

MATH: COMPUTATION

● **Lesson 15: Multiplying and Dividing Fractions (cont.)**

12. $\frac{5}{6} \times \frac{3}{10} = \square$

    (F) $\frac{1}{2}$

    (G) $1\frac{2}{15}$

    (H) $2\frac{7}{9}$

    (J) $\frac{1}{4}$

13. **What is the area of a rectangle that is** $6\frac{1}{2}$ **by** $2\frac{1}{2}$ **?**

    (A) 9 square units

    (B) $16\frac{1}{4}$ square units

    (C) $12\frac{1}{4}$ square units

    (D) $18\frac{3}{4}$ square units

14. **Multiplying** $\frac{3}{5}$ **by which fraction will result in a product less than** $\frac{3}{5}$ **?**

    (F) $\frac{7}{4}$

    (G) $\frac{8}{8}$

    (H) $\frac{9}{10}$

    (J) $1\frac{1}{2}$

15. $4\frac{1}{6} \div 5 = \square$

    (A) $\frac{5}{6}$

    (B) $9\frac{1}{6}$

    (C) $1\frac{1}{6}$

    (D) $\frac{4}{5}$

16. $8 \div \frac{2}{3} = \square$

    (F) $7\frac{1}{3}$

    (G) $5\frac{1}{3}$

    (H) 12

    (J) $8\frac{2}{3}$

17. **Six people share a bag of 57 peanuts equally. Between what two numbers is the amount each person gets?**

    (A) 10 and 11 peanuts

    (B) 11 and 12 peanuts

    (C) 8 and 9 peanuts

    (D) 9 and 10 peanuts

18. **There are 7 boxes stacked on top of one another. Each box is** $9\frac{1}{2}$ **inches tall. How tall is the stack of boxes?**

    (F) $63\frac{1}{2}$ inches

    (G) $66\frac{1}{2}$ inches

    (H) $16\frac{1}{2}$ inches

    (J) $23\frac{1}{2}$ inches

19. $\frac{6}{7} \times \square = \frac{6}{7}$

    (A) $1\frac{2}{3}$

    (B) $\frac{9}{2}$

    (C) $\frac{5}{5}$

    (D) $\frac{3}{4}$

STOP

MATH: COMPUTATION

● Lesson 16: Adding and Subtracting Decimals and Percents

Directions: Solve each problem. Fill in the circle for the correct answer. Choose "None of these" if the correct answer is not given.

Examples

A. 50.25 + 45.36 =

- (A) 9,561
- (B) 95.61
- (C) 956.1
- (D) None of these

B. 47% − 29% =

- (F) 28%
- (G) 18%
- (H) 15%
- (J) None of these

 Clue When adding and subtracting decimals, always make sure that the decimal points are lined up correctly before you begin to solve the problem.

● Practice

1. 48.3 + 6.7 =

- (A) 115.3
- (B) 54.1
- (C) 55
- (D) None of these

2.
   0.583
 − 0.79

- (F) .662
- (G) 1.373
- (H) 1.381
- (J) None of these

3.
   38.03
 − 15.6

- (A) 22.43
- (B) 36.47
- (C) 23
- (D) None of these

4.
$49.39 − $12.87 =

- (F) $36.51
- (G) $37.54
- (H) $35.53
- (J) None of these

5.
27.03% + 39.65% =

- (A) 63.27%
- (B) 56.69%
- (C) 66.68%
- (D) None of these

6.
   50.25%
 − 29.76%

- (F) 77%
- (G) 87%
- (H) 81%
- (J) None of these

STOP

MATH: COMPUTATION

● Lesson 17: Multiplying and Dividing Decimals and Percents

Directions: Solve each problem. Fill in the circle for the correct answer. Choose "None of these" if the correct answer is not given.

Examples

A.	3.6		A	2.16	B.	13% of 4 =	F	0.52
	x 6		B	216			G	0.50
			C	21.6			H	0.59
			D	None of these			J	None of these

 To determine the decimal point in the product (the answer for a multiplication problem), count the number of decimal places in the factors.

● Practice

1.	6.87 x 4 =	A	27.48	4.	12% of 6 =	F	0.84
		B	2.748			G	0.96
		C	274.8			H	0.72
		D	None of these			J	None of these

2.	2.03	F	0.406	5.	34% of 2 =	A	0.36
	x 0.02	G	0.0406			B	0.70
		H	2.006			C	0.66
		J	None of these			D	None of these

3.	3)7.2	A	2.4	6.	37% ÷ 5 =	F	8.6%
		B	2 R12			G	7.4%
		C	2.89			H	6.5%
		D	None of these			J	None of these

STOP

MATH: COMPUTATION
SAMPLE TEST

Directions: Solve each problem. Fill in the circle for the correct answer. Choose "None of these" if the correct answer is not given.

Examples

A. 109 + 356 + 498 + 253 =

- Ⓐ 1,206
- Ⓑ 1,358
- Ⓒ 1,216
- Ⓓ None of these

B. 0.33 x 2.4 =

- Ⓕ 0.792
- Ⓖ 0.927
- Ⓗ 0.872
- Ⓙ None of these

1.
$$1,222$$
$$2,907$$
$$5,745$$
$$+ \; 4,306$$

- Ⓐ 14,270
- Ⓑ 14,320
- Ⓒ 14,180
- Ⓓ None of these

2.
$$7\frac{1}{5} - 5\frac{1}{4} =$$

- Ⓕ $1\frac{2}{5}$
- Ⓖ $2\frac{1}{20}$
- Ⓗ $1\frac{19}{20}$
- Ⓙ None of these

3.
$$24\,\overline{)1,246}$$

- Ⓐ 50 R23
- Ⓑ 52 R16
- Ⓒ 51 R20
- Ⓓ None of these

4.
$$1.576$$
$$+ \; 2.33$$

- Ⓕ 4.102
- Ⓖ 3.906
- Ⓗ 3.889
- Ⓙ None of these

5.
$$3,006$$
$$- \; 1,549$$

- Ⓐ 1,457
- Ⓑ 2,007
- Ⓒ 1,896
- Ⓓ None of these

6.
$$9\,\overline{)310.5}$$

- Ⓕ 36.1
- Ⓖ 35.9
- Ⓗ 34.5
- Ⓙ None of these

7.
$$1\frac{1}{2}$$
$$+ \; 2\frac{3}{4}$$

- Ⓐ $3\frac{1}{2}$
- Ⓑ $4\frac{1}{4}$
- Ⓒ $5\frac{4}{6}$
- Ⓓ None of these

8.
$$303$$
$$+ \; 26$$

- Ⓕ 330
- Ⓖ 328
- Ⓗ 327
- Ⓙ None of these

GO ON

9.
36% + 27% =

(A) 63%
(B) 75%
(C) 61%
(D) None of these

14.
68.4% − 55.7% =

(F) 12.7%
(G) 13.9%
(H) 11.4%
(J) None of these

10.
439 ÷ 6 =

(F) 75 R2
(G) 74 R3
(H) 73 R1
(J) None of these

15.   14% of 6

(A) 0.69
(B) 0.78
(C) 0.84
(D) None of these

11.
1,999 + 463 + 275 =

(A) 2,737
(B) 3,892
(C) 2,688
(D) None of these

16.   3,268
x 135

(F) 441,180
(G) 440,286
(H) 444,223
(J) None of these

12.
99% ÷ 33 =

(F) 6%
(G) 3%
(H) 4 R1
(J) None of these

17.
5,032 − 3,659 =

(A) 1,377
(B) 1,273
(C) 1,337
(D) None of these

13.
4.968
+ 0.554

(A) 5.443
(B) 5.524
(C) 5.522
(D) None of these

18.   7.03
x 6.2

(F) 43.968
(G) 43.586
(H) 43.685
(J) None of these

STOP

Name _____   Date_____

● **Lesson 18: Geometry**

Directions: Fill in the circle for the correct answer to each geometry problem.

> **Example**

A. **The area of the figure to the right is —**

(A) 1,450 square units

(B) 100 square units

(C) 525 square units

(D) 50 square units

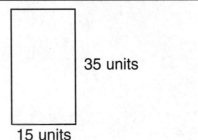

35 units

15 units

 Clue When you are not sure of an answer choice, eliminate the choices you know are wrong. Then take your best guess.

● **Practice**

For numbers 1–3, find the area of each figure.

For numbers 4 and 5, find the perimeter of each figure.

1.

(A) 20 square feet

(B)   8 square feet

(C) 16 square feet

(D) 12 square feet

4 feet

4 feet

4.

(F) 13 meters

(G) 42 meters

(H) 26 meters

(J) 52 meters

7 m

6 m

2.

(F) 15 square centimeters

(G)   8 square centimeters

(H) 16 square centimeters

(J)   4 square centimeters

3 cm

5 cm

5.

(A) 42 yards

(B) 52 yards

(C) 43 yards

(D) 57 yards

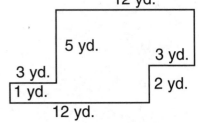

12 yd.

5 yd.

3 yd.

3 yd.

1 yd.

2 yd.

12 yd.

3.

(A) 42 square inches

(B) 21 square inches

(C) 108 square inches

(D) 54 square inches

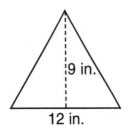

9 in.

12 in.

6. **Look at the circle. What does the line segment AB represent?**

(F) radius

(G) diameter

(H) perimeter

(J) volume

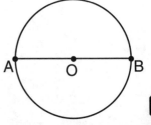

A   O   B

STOP

MATH: APPLICATIONS

● Lesson 19: Geometry

Directions: Fill in the circle for the correct answer to each geometry problem.

Example

A. Which of the following is not a correct name for the angle shown?

Ⓐ ∠ A

Ⓑ ∠ C

Ⓒ ∠ CAB

Ⓓ ∠ BAC

 Clue Look carefully for key words, pictures, and numbers to help you answer the questions.

● Practice

1. What is the measurement of a straight angle?

    Ⓐ 78°

    Ⓑ 25°

    Ⓒ 90°

    Ⓓ 180°

2. Which of the following figures shows at least one right angle?

Ⓕ

Ⓖ

Ⓗ

Ⓙ

3. Which of these is an obtuse angle?

Ⓐ

Ⓑ

Ⓒ

Ⓓ

4. What is the name for this type of angle?

    Ⓕ obtuse

    Ⓖ straight

    Ⓗ right

    Ⓙ acute

STOP

━━━━━━━━━━━━━ MATH: APPLICATIONS ━━━━━━━━━━━━━

● **Lesson 20: Geometry**

Directions: Fill in the circle for the correct answer to each geometry problem.

Examples

Which figure is symmetrical?

A.
- Ⓐ J
- Ⓑ P
- Ⓒ G
- Ⓓ T

B. Which of these shows a ray?

- Ⓕ ○
- Ⓖ △
- Ⓗ ●——→ A B
- Ⓙ ←—→ X Y

Clue Be sure to consider all of the answer choices before making your decision.

● **Practice**

1. **How many pairs of lines below are parallel?**

- Ⓐ one
- Ⓑ two
- Ⓒ three
- Ⓓ four

2. **Look at the coordinate grid. Which sequence of ordered pairs would allow you to move from the school to the library?**

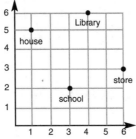

- Ⓕ (2,3), (3,3), (4,3), (5,3), (6,3), (6,4)
- Ⓖ (3,2), (3,3), (3,4), (3,5), (2,5), (1,5)
- Ⓗ (3,2), (3,3), (3,4), (3,5), (3,6), (4,6)
- Ⓙ (2,3), (2,4), (2,5), (2,6), (3,6), (4,6)

3. **How many faces does a cube have?**

- Ⓐ 2
- Ⓑ 4
- Ⓒ 6
- Ⓓ 8

4. **Which pair of shapes is congruent?**

- Ⓕ A
- Ⓖ B
- Ⓗ C
- Ⓙ D

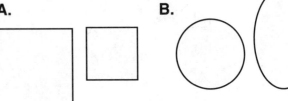

A.

B.

C.

D.

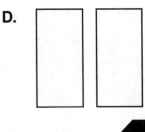

STOP

MATH: APPLICATIONS

● Lesson 21: Geometry

Directions: Fill in the circle for the correct answer to each geometry problem.

Examples

A. A basketball is shaped like a —

- Ⓐ cylinder.
- Ⓑ sphere.
- Ⓒ cube.
- Ⓓ rectangular prism.

B. Which statement is true about line segment AB?

- Ⓕ It extends infinitely in both directions.
- Ⓖ It cannot be measured.
- Ⓗ It is the same as line segment BA.
- Ⓙ It is the same as line AB.

Clue Look carefully at each answer choice before making your decision. Once you have marked your answer, do not change it unless you are certain you made a mistake.

● Practice

1. What type of movement do the figures in the grid below indicate?

- Ⓐ flip
- Ⓑ turn
- Ⓒ slide
- Ⓓ rotate

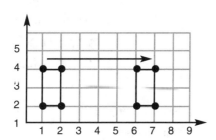

2. Which numbered rectangle is similar to rectangle A?

- Ⓕ rectangle 1
- Ⓖ rectangle 2
- Ⓗ rectangle 3
- Ⓙ rectangle 4

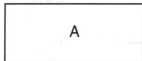

3. Below is a code. Use the code to figure out what word is spelled by the shapes in the box.

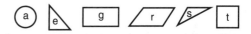

- Ⓐ stars
- Ⓑ great
- Ⓒ greet
- Ⓓ treat

4. Which of the following statements is true about the radius of a circle?

- Ⓕ The radius is the distance around the circle.
- Ⓖ The radius is a line that connects two points on a circle and passes through the center.
- Ⓗ The radius is half the length of the diameter.
- Ⓙ There is only one radius in a circle.

MATH: APPLICATIONS

● **Lesson 22: Classifying Two-Dimensional Figures**

Directions: Choose the best answer for each question.

Examples

A. Which best describes a quadrilateral with 4 congruent sides?

- (A) rhombus
- (B) rectangle
- (C) square
- (D) trapezoid

B. Which describes a shape that is never a rectangle?

- (F) parallelogram
- (G) hexagon
- (H) rhombus
- (J) square

● **Practice**

1. Which describes all trapezoids?

- (A) parallelogram
- (B) rhombus
- (C) quadrilateral
- (D) kite

2. Which best describes a quadrilateral with 2 pairs of parallel sides?

- (F) parallelogram
- (G) rectangle
- (H) rhombus
- (J) square

3. Which describes a shape that is not a polygon?

- (A) circle
- (B) triangle
- (C) square
- (D) pentagon

4. Which is true?

- (F) All rectangles are rhombuses.
- (G) All quadrilaterals are parallelograms.
- (H) All rhombuses are squares.
- (J) All rectangles are parallelograms.

5. Which word is not used to classify triangles?

- (A) right
- (B) obtuse
- (C) parallel
- (D) scalene

6. Which best describes rectangles?

- (F) They have 2 pairs of parallel sides.
- (G) They have 4 right angles.
- (H) They have 2 pairs of congruent sides.
- (J) They have 4 congruent sides.

STOP

MATH: APPLICATIONS

● Lesson 23: Measurement

Directions: Solve each problem. Fill in the circle for the correct answer.

Examples

A. Regina has $2.33 in coins. She has 6 quarters, 5 dimes, 2 nickels, and the rest in pennies. How many pennies does Regina have?

- Ⓐ 12
- Ⓑ 33
- Ⓒ 17
- Ⓓ 23

B. Baxter begins his guitar lesson at 3:00. His lesson lasts for 45 minutes. Before going home, he plays basketball for 35 minutes. It will take him 20 minutes to walk home. At what time will Baxter arrive at home?

- Ⓕ 4:55
- Ⓖ 4:40
- Ⓗ 5:15
- Ⓙ 5:05

 Clue Draw pictures to help solve the problems.

● Practice

1. Scott and Thelma have a dog-walking business. They earn $0.75 every 15 minutes for each dog that they walk. If they take 5 dogs on a 1-hour walk, how much money will they earn?

- Ⓐ $3.75
- Ⓑ $11.00
- Ⓒ $15.00
- Ⓓ $9.00

2. Isabella buys her lunch at school 4 days a week. Lunch costs $2.25 per day. If Isabella pays for 2 weeks worth of lunches in advance, how much change will she get from a $20 bill?

- Ⓕ $2.00
- Ⓖ $3.75
- Ⓗ $6.50
- Ⓙ $11.00

3. Which of these statements is true?

- Ⓐ 25 dimes = $2.75
- Ⓑ 15 quarters = $4.25
- Ⓒ 100 nickels = $5.00
- Ⓓ 20 quarters = $6.00

4. What time will this clock show in 45 minutes?

- Ⓕ 4:05
- Ⓖ 4:00
- Ⓗ 4:15
- Ⓙ 4:20

MATH: APPLICATIONS

● **Lesson 24: Measurement**

Directions: Solve each problem. Fill in the circle for the correct answer.

Example

A. **Which of these is closest to the length of the pencil?**

   Ⓐ $3\frac{1}{2}$ inches

   Ⓑ $2\frac{1}{2}$ inches

   Ⓒ $2\frac{3}{4}$ inches

   Ⓓ $1\frac{3}{4}$ inches

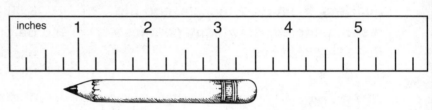

 Clue Look carefully at where objects begin and end on the rulers.

● **Practice**

1. **Which of these is the closest to the length of the sandwich?**

   Ⓐ $5\frac{3}{4}$ inches

   Ⓑ 6 inches

   Ⓒ $6\frac{3}{4}$ inches

   Ⓓ $6\frac{1}{2}$ inches

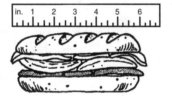

2. **Which of these is the closest to the height of this envelope?**

   Ⓕ 9 cm

   Ⓖ 8.5 cm

   Ⓗ 9.5 cm

   Ⓙ 8 cm

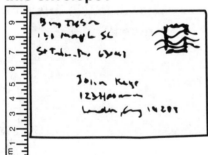

3. **Which of these would be the best unit of measurement to measure a tree?**

   Ⓐ kilometers

   Ⓑ centimeters

   Ⓒ meters

   Ⓓ millimeters

4. **Jeremiah has a photograph that measures 5" x 7". He wants to frame the photograph using a 3-inch mat. What size picture frame will Jeremiah need to accommodate the photograph and mat?**

   Ⓕ 5" x 7"

   Ⓖ 8" x 10"

   Ⓗ 3" x 5"

   Ⓙ 9" x 11"

5. **Eric can throw a ball about 2,300 cm. How many meters can he throw the ball?**

   Ⓐ 2.3 meters

   Ⓑ 23,000 meters

   Ⓒ 230 meters

   Ⓓ 23 meters

6. **About how long is a baseball bat?**

   Ⓕ 3 inches long

   Ⓖ 3 feet long

   Ⓗ 3 yards long

   Ⓙ 3 miles long

STOP

MATH: APPLICATIONS

● Lesson 25: Measurement

Directions: Solve each problem. Fill in the circle for the correct answer.

Examples

A. A football is 11 inches in length. How many footballs would have to be placed end to end to equal more than 1 yard?

- (A) 1
- (B) 2
- (C) 3
- (D) 4

B. Which of these measures is the longest?

- (F) 1 kilometer
- (G) 1 millimeter
- (H) 1 meter
- (J) 1 centimeter

 Clue Sometimes you don't have to compute to find the answer to a problem. For this type of problem, it is especially important to look for key words and numbers that will help you find the answer.

● Practice

1. 1 kilogram =
- (A) 100 milligrams
- (B) 10 grams
- (C) 100 grams
- (D) 1,000 grams

2. Kenny's book is 30 mm thick. How many centimeters thick is the book?
- (F) 0.3 cm
- (G) 3 cm
- (H) 33 cm
- (J) 300 cm

3. About how long is a city block?
- (A) 120 meters
- (B) 55 centimeters
- (C) 48 kilometers
- (D) 100 millimeters

4. A hair comb weighs about 35 grams. How many milligrams does that equal?
- (F) 3.5
- (G) 35,000
- (H) 350
- (J) 3,500

5. Which of these would be the best unit of measurement to measure a ballpoint pen?
- (A) miles
- (B) yards
- (C) inches
- (D) feet

6. A football field is 100 yards long. About how many inches is that?
- (F) 800
- (G) 3,600
- (H) 33
- (J) 400

STOP

MATH: APPLICATIONS

● Lesson 26: Measurement

Directions: Solve each problem. Fill in the circle for the correct answer.

Examples

A. About how much paint is there in a bucket of paint?

- (A) 4 milliliters
- (B) 4 liters
- (C) 4 kiloliters
- (D) 4 cups

B. The graph shows the daily temperature in Mainville City. If the pattern continues, what will the temperature be on Friday?

- (F) 73°
- (G) 68°
- (H) 69°
- (J) 71°

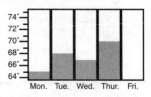

 Clue Use scratch paper to work out the problems. Be sure to transfer the answers correctly.

● Practice

Use the chart to answer numbers 1–3.

1 gallon = 4 quarts	1 quart = 2 pints
1 pint = 2 cups	1 cup = 8 ounces

1. A recipe calls for 6 quarts of water. How many gallons is that?

- (A) 1
- (B) $1\frac{1}{2}$
- (C) 2
- (D) $2\frac{1}{2}$

2. A faucet was leaking water at a rate of 3 cups per day. A total of 9 pints of water leaked from the faucet. How many days did the faucet leak before it was repaired?

- (F) 2 days
- (G) 4 days
- (H) 6 days
- (J) 9 days

3. 4 gallons =

- (A) 40 cups
- (B) 8 quarts
- (C) 16 pints
- (D) 64 cups

4. On the Fahrenheit scale, what is the temperature for the freezing point of water?

- (F) 32°
- (G) 0°
- (H) 57°
- (J) 24°

5. A truck brings fuel oil to school, which is stored in a 12-kiloliter tank. How many liters does the tank hold when it is full?

- (A) 1,200 liters
- (B) 12,000 liters
- (C) 120 liters
- (D) 120,000 liters

STOP

Name _____ Date_____

● **Lesson 27: Volume**

Directions: Find the volume for each figure.

┌─────────────── **Examples** ───────────────┐

A.
Ⓐ 5 cubic units
Ⓑ 6 cubic units
Ⓒ 8 cubic units
Ⓓ 9 cubic units

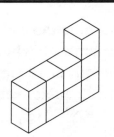

B.
Ⓕ 11 cubic units
Ⓖ 5 cubic units
Ⓗ 9 cubic units
Ⓙ 7 cubic units

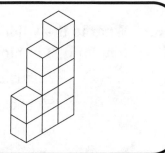

● **Practice**

1.

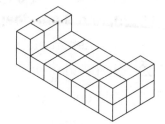

Ⓐ   18 cubic units
Ⓑ   21 cubic units
Ⓒ   27 cubic units
Ⓓ   24 cubic units

2.

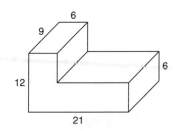

Ⓕ   2,268 cubic units
Ⓖ   1,458 cubic units
Ⓗ   648 cubic units
Ⓙ   1,134 cubic units

3.

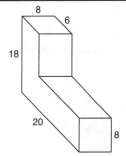

Ⓐ   896 cubic units
Ⓑ   1,376 cubic units
Ⓒ   2,880 cubic units
Ⓓ   1,760 cubic units

4.

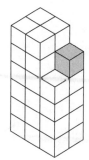

Ⓕ   16 cubic units
Ⓖ   17 cubic units
Ⓗ   32 cubic units
Ⓙ   33 cubic units

GO ON

MATH: APPLICATIONS

● Lesson 27: Volume (cont.)

Directions: Choose the best answer for each question.

5. **What is the volume of a storage unit 6 m long, 3 m high, and 2 m deep?**
   - (A) 72 cubic meters
   - (B) 60 cubic meters
   - (C) 48 cubic meters
   - (D) 36 cubic meters

6. **How many boxes with a volume of 4 cubic meters will fit into a trailer 3 meters high, 4 meters wide, and 9 meters long?**
   - (F) 108 boxes
   - (G) 27 boxes
   - (H) 36 boxes
   - (J) 54 boxes

7. **How tall is a rectangular prism with a volume of 1,728 cubic units and a base with an area of 48 square units?**
   - (A) 12
   - (B) 36
   - (C) 24
   - (D) 48

8. **What is the volume?**
   - (F) 12 cubic units
   - (G) 15 cubic units
   - (H) 13 cubic units
   - (J) 14 cubic units

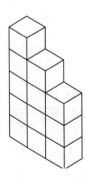

9. **What is the width of a rectangular prism with a height of 8 meters, a length of 12 meters, and a volume of 1,632 cubic meters?**
   - (A) 19 meters
   - (B) 16 meters
   - (C) 18 meters
   - (D) 17 meters

10. **What is the volume of a box 8 cm long, 11 cm high, and 9 cm deep?**
   - (F) 792 cubic centimeters
   - (G) 792 square centimeters
   - (H) 720 cubic centimeters
   - (J) 648 cubic inches

11. **What is the volume?**

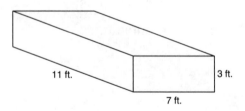

11 ft.   3 ft.   7 ft.

   - (A) 210 cubic feet
   - (B) 252 cubic feet
   - (C) 231 cubic feet
   - (D) 126 cubic feet

STOP

Name _____ Date_____

MATH: APPLICATIONS

● Lesson 28: Problem Solving

Directions: Solve each problem. Fill in the circle for the correct answer. Fill in the circle for "Not given" if your answer is not listed as a choice.

Example

A. Tim's mother is a landscaper. On a new home in the neighborhood, she spent $829 for trees, $358 for flowers, and $352 for a fishpond. How much did she spend on the items for the new yard?

  (A) $1,600
  (B) $1,539
  (C) $1,459
  (D) Not given

 Read each question carefully. Look for key words and numbers to help you decide how to solve the problem.

● Practice

1. A Ferris wheel was built for the Chicago Fair in 1893. In 1904 it was torn down and sold for scrap. How many years did the Ferris wheel run?

  (A) 9 years
  (B) 11 years
  (C) 10 years
  (D) Not given

2. Three friends started a scrapbook business. They charge customers $3.25 per page to make a scrapbook. They spend $1.33 per page on materials. If the friends made a 50-page scrapbook and divided the profits evenly, how much money would each person earn on the project?

  (F) $96.00
  (G) $54.16
  (H) $32.00
  (J) Not given

3. Bert estimates that he will pay about $1,400 a year for his car expenses. He makes $35 every Saturday. How many Saturdays will he need to work to cover his car expenses for 1 year?

  (A) 35
  (B) 40
  (C) 50
  (D) Not given

4. On Monday, Ramona read for 20 minutes. She increased her amount of reading time by 2 minutes a day, every day for 21 days. For how many minutes did Ramona read on the last Sunday during this time?

  (F) 60 minutes
  (G) 56 minutes
  (H) 64 minutes
  (J) Not given

STOP

Name _____ Date_____

● **Lesson 29: Problem Solving**

Directions: Solve each problem. Fill in the circle for the correct answer.

⌐▔▔▔▔▔▔▔ **Example** ▔▔▔▔▔▔▔⌐

There were 4 schools that participated in a district fundraiser. The schools raised a total of $2,500. The graph below shows the percentages that each school contributed to the total amount raised. Use the information in the graph to answer the question.

A. **How much money did Willow School contribute to the fundraiser?**

Ⓐ $750
Ⓑ $250
Ⓒ $625
Ⓓ $875

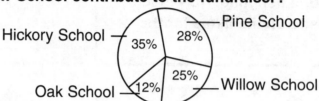

Hickory School — 35%   28% — Pine School
Oak School — 12%   25% — Willow School

 Clue   Make sure you understand what each graph is representing.

● **Practice**

Use this graph to answer questions 1–2.

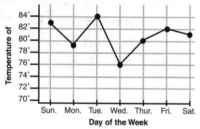

Temperature of
84°
82°
80°
78°
76°
74°
72°
70°
Sun. Mon. Tue. Wed. Thur. Fri. Sat.
Day of the Week

1. **What is the difference between the highest temperature and the lowest temperature shown?**

Ⓐ 1°
Ⓑ 10°
Ⓒ 8°
Ⓓ 12°

2. **Which day has the temperature that is the median temperature of the week?**

Ⓕ Tuesday
Ⓖ Saturday
Ⓗ Friday
Ⓙ Wednesday

Use this table to answer questions 3–4.

	Summer Sale 15% Off	
	Regular Price	Sale Price
Shorts	$15.99	$13.99
Shirts	$12.99	$11.00
Shoes	$45.99	$39.09

3. **Lydia bought 3 pairs of shorts, 4 shirts, and 1 pair of shoes for the advertised sales prices. Assuming there was no tax, how much did she spend?**

Ⓐ $87.35
Ⓑ $145.92
Ⓒ $63.68
Ⓓ $125.06

4. **How much money did Lydia save on her purchase because of the sale?**

Ⓕ $20.86
Ⓖ $25.32
Ⓗ $18.58
Ⓙ $21.73

 STOP

MATH: APPLICATIONS

● **Lesson 30: Problem Solving**

Directions: Solve each problem. Fill in the circle for the correct answer.

Example

A.   In the group of shapes, the odds of picking a square over a triangle are 3 to 1. What are the odds of choosing a circle over a square?

Ⓐ   1 to 5
Ⓑ   3 to 5
Ⓒ   5 to 3
Ⓓ   5 to 1

Clue   Look for patterns to help you solve the problems.

● **Practice**

Use the information in the box to answer numbers 1–2.

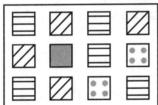

1.   The tiles above are in a bag. If you randomly chose one without looking, which type would you probably choose?

Ⓐ
Ⓑ
Ⓒ
Ⓓ

2.   Which fraction shows the ratio of

 to ?

Ⓕ $\frac{2}{4}$

Ⓖ $\frac{1}{5}$

Ⓗ $\frac{2}{5}$

Ⓙ $\frac{4}{1}$

3.   Which spinner would give you the best chance of landing on the number 2?

Ⓐ
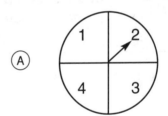

Ⓑ
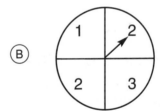

Ⓒ
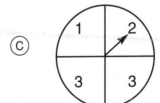

Ⓓ
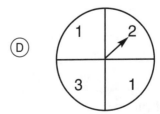

MATH: APPLICATIONS

● **Lesson 31: Problem Solving**

Directions: Solve each problem. Fill in the circle for the correct answer. Fill in the circle for "Not given" if your answer is not listed as a choice.

Examples

A. There are 5 stuffed animals on a shelf. The giraffe is before the dog. There are 2 animals between the dog and the bear. The cat is next to the bear, and the zebra is last. Which sequence shows the order the animals are in?

- (A) giraffe, dog, cat, bear, zebra
- (B) bear, cat, giraffe, dog, zebra
- (C) dog, giraffe, cat, bear, zebra
- (D) Not given

B. Which is an even number that is less than 6,122 but more than 5,998?

- (F) 6,142
- (G) 5,996
- (H) 6,104
- (J) Not given

 Clue Use scratch paper to draw pictures and record information to solve these problems.

● **Practice**

Use the information in the box to answer numbers 1–2.

$A = (D−C) ÷ 2$
$B = A + C$
$C = D ÷ 2$
$D =$ The difference between 20 and 4

1. What is the value of A?
- (A) 4
- (B) 5
- (C) 6
- (D) Not given

2. What is the value of B?
- (F) 9
- (G) 11
- (H) 12
- (J) Not given

Use the information in the box to answer numbers 3 and 4.

Xavier is twice the age of Yvonne.
Yvonne is 3 years younger than Zane.
Zane is 2 years older than Alisa.
Alisa is 6 years old.

3. How many years older is Xavier than Zane?
- (A) 1 year
- (B) 2 years
- (C) 3 years
- (D) Not given

4. Who is the youngest?
- (F) Yvonne
- (G) Alisa
- (H) Zane
- (J) Not given

STOP

MATH: APPLICATIONS

● Lesson 32: Interpreting Data

Directions: Use the line plots to choose the best answers to the questions.

Mr. Riviera measured the amount of spice left in each of his spice jars and recorded the results in the line plot below.

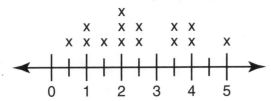

Amount in Spice Jars (tablespoons)

1. If each jar can hold up to 5 tablespoons of spice, how many tablespoons can be added to the emptiest jar?

    Ⓐ $1\frac{1}{2}$ T.

    Ⓑ $4\frac{1}{2}$ T.

    Ⓒ $2\frac{1}{2}$ T.

    Ⓓ $3\frac{1}{2}$ T.

2. How many tablespoons of spices did Mr. Riviera measure in all?

    Ⓕ 35 T.

    Ⓖ 14 T.

    Ⓗ 28 T.

    Ⓙ 21 T.

3. If all the spices are mixed, and the mixture is then distributed evenly back into the jars, how many tablespoons of the spice mix would be in each jar?

    Ⓐ 1 T.

    Ⓑ $1\frac{1}{2}$ T.

    Ⓒ 2 T.

    Ⓓ $2\frac{1}{2}$ T.

Ms. Ronson measured the length of each piece of chalk in her classroom. She recorded the results in the line plot below.

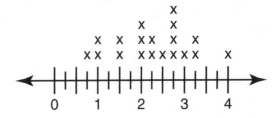

Length of Chalk (inches)

4. What is the difference in the length of the longest and shortest pieces of chalk?

    Ⓕ $2\frac{1}{2}$ inches

    Ⓖ 3 inches

    Ⓗ $2\frac{3}{4}$ inch

    Ⓙ $3\frac{1}{4}$ inch

5. What is the difference in length of the most common length of chalk and the second most common length?

    Ⓐ $1\frac{3}{4}$ inches

    Ⓑ $\frac{1}{4}$ inch

    Ⓒ $\frac{3}{4}$ inch

    Ⓓ $1\frac{1}{4}$ inches

6. If all of the pieces of chalk were put together end to end, about how long would they be in all?

    Ⓕ 30 inches

    Ⓖ 35 inches

    Ⓗ 40 inches

    Ⓙ 50 inches

STOP

MATH: APPLICATIONS

● **Lesson 33: The Coordinate Plane**

Directions: Use the graphs to choose the best answer for each question.

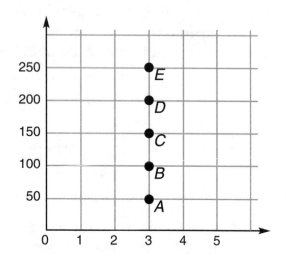

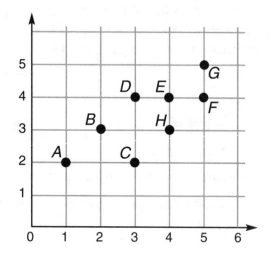

1. **What are the coordinates of point _A_?**
   - (A) (3, 50)
   - (B) (3.5, 55)
   - (C) (3, 100)
   - (D) (300, 50)

2. **What might the coordinates of point _B_ represent?**
   - (F) a car that traveled 50 miles in 3 hours
   - (G) a car that traveled 150 miles in 3 hours
   - (H) a car that traveled 100 miles in 3 hours
   - (J) a car that traveled 250 miles in 3 hours

3. **Which point represents coordinates (3, 200)?**
   - (A) point _E_
   - (B) point _D_
   - (C) point _C_
   - (D) point _A_

4. **What are the coordinates of point _B_?**
   - (F) (3, 2)
   - (G) (1, 2)
   - (H) (2, 3)
   - (J) (3, 4)

5. **Which point represents coordinates (4, 3)?**
   - (A) point _E_
   - (B) point _G_
   - (C) point _H_
   - (D) point _F_

6. **What might the coordinates of point _A_ represent?**
   - (F) a person who hiked 2 miles in 2 hours
   - (G) a person who hiked 2 miles in 1 hour
   - (H) a person who hiked 1 mile for 4 hours
   - (J) a person who hiked 2 miles for 6 hours

STOP

142

Name _____   Date_____

MATH: APPLICATIONS
SAMPLE TEST

Directions: Solve each problem. Fill in the circle for the correct answer.

Examples

A. About how much do 2 paper clips weigh?

- Ⓐ 1 gram
- Ⓑ 1 pound
- Ⓒ 1 kilogram
- Ⓓ 1 ounce

B. Two lines that do not intersect and are the same distance apart at every point are said to be —

- Ⓕ congruent.
- Ⓖ parallel.
- Ⓗ right angles.
- Ⓙ perpendicular.

---

1. Which 2 line segments are congruent?

- Ⓐ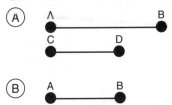
- Ⓑ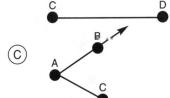
- Ⓒ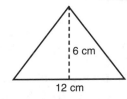
- Ⓓ

2. What is the area of this triangle?

6 cm

12 cm

- Ⓕ 72 square centimeters
- Ⓖ 48 square centimeters
- Ⓗ 36 square centimeters
- Ⓙ 18 square centimeters

3. Lincoln School is hosting a dinner for its honor students. There will be 50 students at the dinner. If 4 chairs fit around 1 table, how many tables will be needed for the students?

- Ⓐ 12
- Ⓑ 13
- Ⓒ 14
- Ⓓ 15

4. The figure below is a sketch showing the cafeteria at Lincoln School. If you walked completely around the cafeteria, about how far would you go?

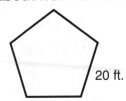

20 ft.

- Ⓕ 100 ft.
- Ⓖ 80 ft.
- Ⓗ 120 ft.
- Ⓙ 400 ft.

GO ON

978-1-62057-597-0 *Spectrum Test Practice 5*

MATH: APPLICATIONS
SAMPLE TEST (cont.)

5. This clock shows the time Tina's soccer game ended. It took 15 minutes to help pack up the equipment and then 20 minutes to arrive at the pizza parlor. At what time did Tina and her teammates arrive at the pizza parlor?

- (A) 4:50
- (B) 5:05
- (C) 4:55
- (D) 5:00

6. The art teacher is paid $15 per hour. She works for 6 hours a day. Which number sentence shows how to find the amount she earns in 1 day?

- (F) 15 + 6 = ○
- (G) 15 − 6 = ○
- (H) 15 x 6 = ○
- (J) 15 ÷ 6 = ○

7. What is the volume of this figure?

- (A) 18 cubic units
- (B) 192 cubic units
- (C) 32 cubic units
- (D) 48 cubic units

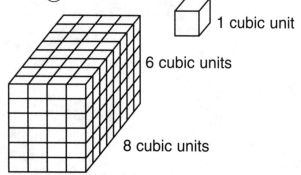

1 cubic unit

6 cubic units

8 cubic units

8. Glen is planting a flower garden in the shape of a triangle. He has placed 80 meters of fencing around the garden. Two sides of the garden are the same length, 25 meters. What is the length of the third side?

- (F) 30 meters
- (G) 40 meters
- (H) 25 meters
- (I) 50 meters

A survey on favorite colors was taken at Rosa's school. The graph below shows the results of the survey. Study the graph, then answer numbers 9 and 10.

 = 5 people

= blue
= red
= yellow

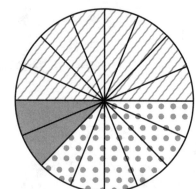

9. How many students chose blue as their favorite color?

- (A) 8
- (B) 50
- (C) 24
- (D) 40

10. How many more students prefer the color red over yellow?

- (F) 4
- (G) 12
- (H) 20
- (J) 35

GO ON

MATH: APPLICATIONS
SAMPLE TEST (cont.)

Store	12 Prints	24 Prints	36 Prints	Double Prints
Thrift Mart	$4.99	$6.99	$8.99	$0.05 each
Food and Go	$3.00	$6.00	$9.00	$0.04 each
Photo Store	$5.25	$7.50	$9.75	$0.07 each
Save More	$3.75	$6.50	$10.25	$0.06 each

The chart above shows the cost of printing photos at different places. Study the chart, then do numbers 11–13.

11. At which store would you get the best price for 12 prints and 36 prints?
    - Ⓐ Thrift Mart
    - Ⓑ Food and Go
    - Ⓒ Photo Store
    - Ⓓ Save More

12. How much would it cost for 24 prints at Save More if you ordered double prints of everything on three different visits?
    - Ⓕ $18.09
    - Ⓖ $24.73
    - Ⓗ $19.50
    - Ⓙ $23.82

13. Photo Store is having a sale. After buying 24 prints on 3 visits, you receive a 50% discount on your fourth order of 24 prints. What will be your total cost for visiting the store 10 times and buying 24 prints each time?
    - Ⓐ $62.80
    - Ⓑ $63.75
    - Ⓒ $67.50
    - Ⓓ $68.45

14. On Monday, Jeremy took 20 minutes to wash the dishes. On Tuesday, Tracy took $\frac{1}{4}$ hour to wash the dishes. On Wednesday, Matthew took $\frac{2}{5}$ hour to wash the dishes. On Thursday, Danielle took $\frac{1}{5}$ hour to wash the dishes. Which person took the least amount of time to wash the dishes?
    - Ⓕ Jeromy
    - Ⓖ Tracy
    - Ⓗ Matthew
    - Ⓙ Danielle

15. Mrs. Hammersmith's fifth grade class took a science test. There are 32 students in the class. The class scored a total of 2,848 points on the test. What was the average score?
    - Ⓐ 89
    - Ⓑ 92
    - Ⓒ 73
    - Ⓓ 87

16. Wendy earns an allowance of $12 per week. She wants to buy a bicycle that will cost $99.72. How many weeks will Wendy need to save her allowance to have enough to buy the bicycle?
    - Ⓕ 7
    - Ⓖ 8
    - Ⓗ 9
    - Ⓙ 10

Use this graph to answer questions 17–20.

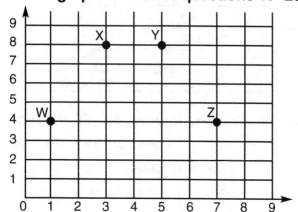

17. What point is at (5,8)?

- (A) W
- (B) X
- (C) Y
- (D) Z

18. How would you have to move to go from point W to point X?

- (F) -2 units horizontally, +4 units vertically
- (G) -2 units horizontally, -4 units vertically
- (H) +2 units horizontally, -4 units vertically
- (J) +2 units horizontally, +4 units vertically

19. If you connected points W and X, points X and Y, points Y and Z, and points Z and W, what shape would you have?

- (A) a rhombus
- (B) a trapezoid
- (C) a hexagon
- (D) a pentagon

20. If you moved one unit at a time and did not move diagonally, which two of the following points would be the farthest from each other?

- (F) W and Y
- (G) Y and Z
- (H) W and Z
- (J) W and X

21. Which shape contains the most angles?

- (A) a quadrilateral
- (B) a hexagon
- (C) a pentagon
- (D) an octagon

22. Which of these does not show a line of symmetry?

- (F)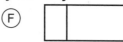
- (G)
- (H)
- (J)

23. What is an odd number that is less than 7,983 and more than 6,735?

- (A) 6,659
- (B) 7,989
- (C) 7,827
- (D) 6,573

STOP

MATH PRACTICE TEST

● **Part 1: Math Concepts**

Directions: Read each problem. Fill in the circle for the correct answer.

Examples

A. Which statement is true about the group of numbers below?

| 21, 35, 42, 63, 84 |

- Ⓐ They are all multiples of 3.
- Ⓑ They are all multiples of 7.
- Ⓒ They are all multiples of 8.
- Ⓓ They are all multiples of 9.

B. Which of these numerals is greater than the Roman numeral VII?

- Ⓕ IX
- Ⓖ III
- Ⓗ IV
- Ⓙ V

1. Which group of decimals is ordered from least to greatest?

- Ⓐ 3.332, 3.321, 3.295, 3.287, 3.111
- Ⓑ 3.424, 3.425, 3.339, 3.383, 3.214
- Ⓒ 3.109, 3.107, 3.278, 3.229, 3.344
- Ⓓ 3.132, 3.234, 3.262, 3.391, 3.406

2. Which of these is even and cannot be divided evenly by 6?

- Ⓕ 28
- Ⓖ 30
- Ⓗ 35
- Ⓙ 42

3. $\sqrt{64} =$

- Ⓐ 12
- Ⓑ 9
- Ⓒ 8
- Ⓓ 7

4. One hundred fourteen thousand, two hundred =

- Ⓕ 1,014,200
- Ⓖ 11,420
- Ⓗ 114,002
- Ⓙ 114,200

5. Three students collected cans of food for a local food drive. The first student collected 78 cans, the second student collected 66 cans, and the third student collected 63 cans. If they rounded the number of cans to nearest ten and added them together, what number would they get?

- Ⓐ 206
- Ⓑ 210
- Ⓒ 200
- Ⓓ 190

6. Forty-two thousand, six hundred seventy-seven =

- Ⓕ 420,677
- Ⓖ 40,267
- Ⓗ 24,767
- Ⓙ 42,677

7. Which of these is true?

- Ⓐ $\frac{5}{8} > \frac{6}{9}$
- Ⓑ $\frac{2}{3} < \frac{3}{4}$
- Ⓒ $\frac{5}{10} = \frac{9}{11}$
- Ⓓ $\frac{4}{5} > \frac{5}{4}$

GO ON ⇨

MATH PRACTICE TEST
Part 1: Math Concepts (cont.)

8. 49 =

    (F) 7^2

    (G) 6^2

    (H) 7^7

    (J) 8^5

9. **What are all of the factors of the product 8 times 3?**

    (A) 2, 4, 6, 8, 10, 12

    (B) 1, 2, 4, 8, 12

    (C) 1, 2, 3, 4, 6, 8, 12, 24

    (D) 1, 2, 3, 4, 5, 6, 7, 8

10. **Which number sentence goes in the same fact family as 6 x 3 = ◯?**

    (F) $3 \times ◯ = 6$

    (G) $◯ \div 3 = 6$

    (H) $3 + ◯ = 6$

    (J) $◯ - 3 = 6$

11. **Suppose you replaced the number 5 in 50,692 with an 8. How much larger would the new number be?**

    (A) 50,000

    (B) 10,000

    (C) 30,000

    (D) 3,000

12. **What number should go in both boxes to make these number sentences true?**

$$□ - 9 = 27$$
$$6 \times 6 = □$$

    (F) 36

    (G) 30

    (H) 42

    (J) 39

13. **Which of these is a prime number?**

    (A) 75

    (B) 25

    (C) 13

    (D) 21

14. **On the number line below, which letter is closest to 3.8?**

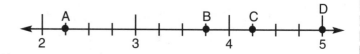

    (F) A

    (G) B

    (H) C

    (J) D

15. **What symbol should go in both boxes to make this number sentence true?**

$$48 □ 6 = 8 □ 1$$

    (A) +

    (B) −

    (C) x

    (D) ÷

16. **Look at the table below. The numbers in row A follow a rule to create the numbers in row B. What is the missing number in row B?**

A	3	5	7	9	11
B	5	9	13		21

    (F) 15

    (G) 17

    (H) 11

    (J) 19

STOP

MATH PRACTICE TEST

● Part 2: Computation

Directions: Solve each problem. Fill in the circle for the correct answer. Choose "None of these" if the correct answer is not given.

Examples

A. $6 - \dfrac{2}{3} =$
- (A) $5\dfrac{2}{3}$
- (B) $5\dfrac{1}{3}$
- (C) 5
- (D) None of these

B. $4 \times 5 \times 6 =$
- (F) 120
- (G) 130
- (H) 110
- (J) None of these

---

1. $9 \times 3.5 =$
- (A) 27.15
- (B) 30.9
- (C) 32.5
- (D) None of these

2.
$$\begin{array}{r} 23.54 \\ -\ 0.26 \\ \hline \end{array}$$
- (F) 22.83
- (G) 23.28
- (H) 23.32
- (J) None of these

3.
$574 + 44 + 3,996 =$
- (A) 4,614
- (B) 5,321
- (C) 4,782
- (D) None of these

4.
$58\,\overline{)\,348}$
- (F) 8
- (G) 4
- (H) 12
- (J) None of these

5.
$$\begin{array}{r} 7,302 \\ +\ 6,528 \\ \hline \end{array}$$
- (A) 138,210
- (B) 13,830
- (C) 14,388
- (D) None of these

6.
$\dfrac{1}{4} \times 36 =$
- (F) 8
- (G) 12
- (H) 9
- (J) None of these

7. $3\,\overline{)\,47}$
- (A) 14
- (B) 16 R1
- (C) 15 R2
- (D) None of these

8.
$10,030 - 2,856 =$
- (F) 7,174
- (G) 6,741
- (H) 8,224
- (J) None of these

9.
$4\dfrac{5}{6} - \dfrac{2}{3} =$
- (A) $4\dfrac{1}{3}$
- (B) $3\dfrac{2}{3}$
- (C) $3\dfrac{4}{6}$
- (D) None of these

10. $2,468 \div 6 =$
- (F) 410 R4
- (G) 411 R2
- (H) 411 R5
- (J) None of these

GO ON

978-1-62057-597-0 *Spectrum Test Practice 5*

MATH PRACTICE TEST
Part 2: Computation (cont.)

11. $585 \div 9 =$
- (A) 69
- (B) 66 R3
- (C) 65
- (D) None of these

12.
$$6\frac{7}{8}$$
$$+ 3\frac{4}{5}$$
- (F) $10\frac{7}{40}$
- (G) $10\frac{3}{8}$
- (H) $10\frac{2}{5}$
- (J) None of these

13. $0.09 \times 90 =$
- (A) 810
- (B) 81
- (C) 8.1
- (D) None of these

14.
$$\$15.43$$
$$+ \ 0.78$$
- (F) $16.22
- (G) $15.91
- (H) $16.38
- (J) None of these

15.
$$28$$
$$566$$
$$4$$
$$+ 1,927$$
- (A) 2,763
- (B) 3,968
- (C) 2,525
- (D) None of these

16. $13.7 + 4.5 =$
- (F) 18.2
- (G) 18.3
- (H) 19.1
- (J) None of these

17.
$$336$$
$$\times \ 407$$
- (A) 163,275
- (B) 136,527
- (C) 136,752
- (D) None of these

18.
$$\frac{5}{9}$$
$$+ \quad \frac{2}{3}$$
- (F) $1\frac{5}{18}$
- (G) $1\frac{2}{9}$
- (H) $\frac{7}{12}$
- (J) None of these

19. $7\overline{)\,4,431}$
- (A) 630
- (B) 632 R7
- (C) 631 R9
- (D) None of these

20.
$$3\frac{4}{15}$$
$$+ \quad \frac{6}{15}$$
- (F) $3\frac{1}{5}$
- (G) $3\frac{2}{15}$
- (H) $3\frac{2}{3}$
- (J) None of these

21.
$$\frac{3}{8}$$
$$+ \quad \frac{2}{10}$$
- (A) $\frac{5}{2}$
- (B) $\frac{23}{40}$
- (C) $\frac{7}{10}$
- (D) None of these

STOP

— MATH PRACTICE TEST —

● Part 3: Math Applications

Directions: Read each problem. Fill in the circle for the correct answer.

Examples

A. Which of these shapes has 6 faces?

- Ⓐ cube
- Ⓑ rectangle
- Ⓒ pyramid
- Ⓓ hexagon

B. How do you find the perimeter of a rectangle?

- Ⓕ square the length of one side
- Ⓖ subtract the length of the shortest side from the length of the longest side
- Ⓗ multiply the base times the height
- Ⓙ add the lengths of all sides

---

1. This clock shows the time that a family arrived at a campground. It took the family 3.25 hours to drive from their home to a restaurant. They took 0.75 hours to eat lunch and then drove for another 2.5 hours. At what time did the family leave their home?

- Ⓐ 9:15
- Ⓑ 8:45
- Ⓒ 8:30
- Ⓓ 9:00

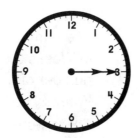

2. A factory shipped 848 cars to 8 cities. Each city received the same number of cars. How many cars were shipped to each city?

- Ⓕ 112
- Ⓖ 108
- Ⓗ 101
- Ⓙ 106

3. Maria is making a video recording for a family history project. She plans to record 30 minutes of live action herself. Her parents have agreed to provide her with twice as much footage from the past as the live action she plans to shoot. Her grandparents have given her a recording they had made for their 50th wedding anniversary. That video runs $\frac{3}{4}$ the length of time of the footage Maria's parents will give her. How long will Maria's recording be after she puts all of the pieces together?

- Ⓐ 2 hours, 30 minutes
- Ⓑ 2 hours, 15 minutes
- Ⓒ 3 hours, 5 minutes
- Ⓓ 3 hours, 45 minutes

4. What is the best way to describe the figure below?

- Ⓕ parallel lines
- Ⓖ perpendicular lines
- Ⓗ obtuse angles
- Ⓙ acute angles

GO ON

5. Brian made a fruit salad. He included 6 cups of raspberries, 4 cups of grapes, 3 cups of chopped pears, and 1 cup of sliced bananas. What is the ratio of raspberries to bananas?

   (A) 4 to 6
   (B) 6 to 2
   (C) 1 to 3
   (D) 6 to 1

6. A rectangular prism is 4 units wide, 10 units long, and 3 units high. What is its volume?

   (F) 17 cubic units
   (G) 120 cubic units
   (H) 102 cubic units
   (J) 60 cubic units

7. What number sentence shows the perimeter of the square below?

   (A) 4 + 25 = □
   (B) 252 = □
   (C) 4 x 25 = □
   (D) 25 x 25 x 25 x 25 = □

   25m

8. For the first 26 weeks of this year, Kendra watched 546 hours of television. In the next 13 weeks, she cut her television time in half. During the last 13 weeks of the year, she cut that time in half again. By the end of the year, what was the average amount of television that Kendra watched per day?

   (F) 55 minutes
   (G) 2 hours, 37 minutes
   (H) 1 hour, 30 minutes
   (J) 45 minutes

The graph below shows the number of books that were donated to a children's hospital each week for a month. Study the graph, then answer questions 9–10.

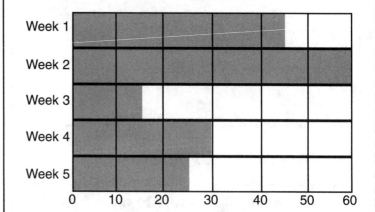

9. Which of the following statements is true?

   (A) There were twice as many books collected in Week 2 than in Week 1.
   (B) The number of books collected in Weeks 3 and 4 is equal to the number of books collected in Week 2.
   (C) There were twice as many books collected in Week 1 than in Week 4.
   (D) There were 3 times the number of books collected in Week 1 than in Week 3.

10. How many books were collected in all?

   (F) 125
   (G) 150
   (H) 175
   (J) 190

GO ON

MATH PRACTICE TEST
Part 3: Math Applications (cont.)

11. Tom's age is an even number less than 14. He is $\frac{1}{2}$ his sister's age. His sister's age is between 16 and 24. How old is Tom?

    (A) 8
    (B) 9
    (C) 10
    (D) 11

12. What is the average length of a side of the figure below?

    (F) 9 cm
    (G) 12 cm
    (H) 8 cm
    (J) 10 cm

6 cm

12 cm

13. In the figure below, the distance between each letter is the same. Which statement about the figure is false?

    L   M   N   O   P

    (A) Distance LP = 4 times Distance MN
    (B) Distance NP = Distance MO
    (C) Distance LN = 2 times Distance OP
    (D) Distance MP = Distance LN

14. At a car manufacturing plant, the workers install about 47 sets of tires on the cars in an hour. Each car has 4 tires. What is the best estimate of the number of tires that are installed in 8 hours?

    (F) 1,500
    (G) 1,600
    (H) 1,700
    (J) 1,800

15. Which of these is the shortest distance?

    (A) 2 miles
    (B) 3 kilometers
    (C) 14 meters
    (D) 500 yards

Three schools, Western Hills, South Middle School, and Willow East, are collecting aluminum cans as part of the school district's recycling effort. Study the graph below, then answer questions 16 and 17.

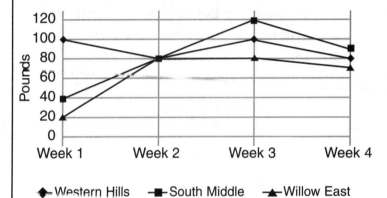

◆ Western Hills   ■ South Middle   ▲ Willow East

16. Which week saw each school collect the same weight of cans?

    (F) Week 1
    (G) Week 2
    (H) Week 3
    (J) Week 4

17. If aluminum cans are currently worth $0.53 per pound at the local recycling station, how much did the 3 schools earn in total?

    (A) $425.30
    (B) $433.70
    (C) $469.40
    (D) $498.20

GO ON

MATH PRACTICE TEST
Part 3: Math Applications (cont.)

18. Juan and Jason have been working on a computer project, and they want to protect their work. They decide to use the sum of all of the prime numbers between 0 and 30 as the password. What is their password?

  (F) 130
  (G) 129
  (H) 112
  (J) 123

19. What is the number sentence for determining the volume of a rectangular prism that measures 3 units long, 5 units wide, and 8 units high?

  (A) $3 \times 5 \times 8 = \square$
  (B) $3 + 5 + 8 = \square$
  (C) $(3 \times 5) + 8 = \square$
  (D) $(3 + 5) \times 8 = \square$

20. A package weighs 18 kilograms. The contents weigh 16.25 kilograms. How much does the container weigh?

  (F) 1.5 kg
  (G) 2.25 kg
  (H) 1,750 g
  (J) 175 g

21. Andrea bought 4 packs of stickers for $3.45 each. If she gave the clerk $20, how much change did she receive?

  (A) $5.20
  (B) $8.20
  (C) $7.20
  (D) $6.20

22. How can the yard lines on a football field be described?

  (F) They are parallel.
  (G) They are perpendicular.
  (H) They intersect.
  (J) They have an infinite length.

Use this graph to answer questions 23 and 24.

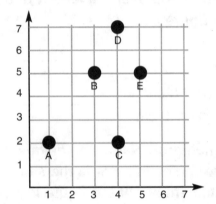

23. What are the coordinates for point D?

  (A) (4, 2)
  (B) (4, 7)
  (C) (5, 5)
  (D) (7, 4)

24. If you connect points A, B, and C, what shape will be formed?

  (F) a sphere
  (G) a square
  (H) a triangular prism
  (J) a triangle

STOP

ANSWER KEY

READING: VOCABULARY

Lesson 1: Synonyms
• Page 7
- **A.** B
- **B.** J
- 1. A
- 2. H
- 3. C
- 4. F
- 5. B
- 6. J
- 7. A
- 8. H

Lesson 2: Vocabulary Skills
• Page 8
- **A.** D
- **B.** G
- 1. A
- 2. J
- 3. B
- 4. F
- 5. D
- 6. H
- 7. C

Lesson 3: Antonyms
• Page 9
- **A.** C
- **B.** F
- 1. A
- 2. J
- 3. A
- 4. H
- 5. B
- 6. J
- 7. A
- 8. G

Lesson 4: Multi-Meaning Words
• Page 10
- **A.** C
- **B.** G
- 1. D
- 2. H
- 3. A

Lesson 5: Words in Context
• Page 11
- **A.** C
- **B.** F
- 1. B
- 2. F
- 3. B
- 4. J
- 5. C
- 6. J

Lesson 6: Word Study
• Page 12
- **A.** A
- **B.** H
- 1. B
- 2. J
- 3. A
- 4. F
- 5. C
- 6. G

Lesson 7: Words From Greek and Latin, Idioms
• Page 13
- **A.** D
- **B.** G
- 1. B
- 2. F
- 3. B
- 4. F

- 5. C
- 6. J

SAMPLE TEST
• Pages 14–17
- **A.** D
- **B.** G
- 1. A
- 2. H
- 3. B
- 4. F
- 5. D
- 6. G
- 7. C
- 8. F
- 9. D
- 10. H
- 11. A
- 12. H
- 13. D
- 14. G
- 15. A
- 16. G
- 17. D
- 18. F
- 19. B
- 20. J
- 21. B
- 22. F
- 23. D
- 24. H
- 25. B
- 26. F
- 27. C
- 28. H
- 29. B
- 30. J
- 31. A
- 32. H
- 33. A
- 34. J
- 35. B

READING: COMPREHENSION

Lesson 8: Main Idea
• Page 18
- **A.** A
- 1. B
- 2. H
- 3. D
- 4. F

Lesson 9: Recalling Details
• Page 19
- **A.** B
- 1. A
- 2. J
- 3. C
- 4. J

Lesson 10: Inferencing and Drawing Conclusions
• Page 20
- **A.** C
- 1. D
- 2. F
- 3. B
- 4. J

Lesson 11: Fact and Opinion/Cause and Effect
• Page 21
- **A.** D
- 1. B
- 2. F
- 3. C

Lesson 12: Fiction
• Pages 22–23
- **A.** C
- 1. B
- 2. F
- 3. D
- 4. J
- 5. B
- 6. H

Lesson 13: Fiction
• Pages 24–25
- **A.** B
- 1. A
- 2. J
- 3. B
- 4. H
- 5. B
- 6. F

Lesson 14: Fiction
• Pages 26–27
- **A.** D
- 1. B
- 2. H
- 3. A
- 4. J
- 5. C
- 6. F

Lesson 15: Reading Literature
• Pages 28–29
- 1. B
- 2. F
- 3. D
- 4. J
- 5. B
- 6. H
- 7. D
- 8. H

Lesson 16: Parts of a Story
• Page 30
- **A.** A
- 1. A
- 2. H
- 3. A
- 4. J

Lesson 17: Nonfiction
• Pages 31–32
- **A.** A
- 1. C
- 2. F
- 3. D
- 4. H
- 5. A
- 6. H

Lesson 18: Nonfiction
• Pages 33–34
- **A.** D
- 1. D
- 2. G
- 3. D
- 4. H
- 5. A
- 6. G

Lesson 19: Nonfiction
• Pages 35–36
- **A.** D
- 1. A
- 2. F
- 3. C
- 4. J
- 5. B
- 6. H

Published by Spectrum. Copyright protected.

978-1-62057-597-0 *Spectrum Test Practice 5*

Lesson 20: Reading Informational Text
• Pages 37–38
1. A
2. G
3. C
4. H
5. C
6. H
7. B
8. J

SAMPLE TEST
• Pages 39–45
A. C
1. B
2. G
3. A
4. J
5. C
6. J
7. A
8. J
9. C
10. H
11. A
12. H
13. B
14. J
15. A
16. J
17. B
18. G
19. A
20. J
21. B
22. H

READING PRACTICE TEST
Part 1: Vocabulary
• Pages 46–48
A. A
B. G
1. D
2. F
3. A
4. J
5. C
6. G
7. A
8. J
9. C
10. F
11. D
12. G
13. D
14. H
15. A
16. G
17. C
18. F
19. A
20. J
21. B

Part 2: Comprehension
• Pages 49–54
A. C
1. D
2. H
3. A
4. G
5. B
6. F
7. B
8. J

9. C
10. F
11. C
12. G
13. D
14. F
15. C
16. G
17. B
18. J
19. C
20. F

LANGUAGE: MECHANICS
Lesson 1: Punctuation
• Page 55
A. B
B. J
1. B
2. H
3. A
4. J
5. B
6. F

Lesson 2: Punctuation
• Page 56
A. B
1. A
2. H
3. B
4. G
5. C
6. F
7. B

Lesson 3: Capitalization and Punctuation
• Page 57
A. C
B. F
1. B
2. J
3. D
4. G
5. C

Lesson 4: Capitalization and Punctuation
• Page 58
A. A
1. C
2. F
3. B
4. G
5. D
6. F

Lesson 5: Capitalization and Punctuation
• Page 59
A. B
B. J
1. D
2. F
3. B
4. H
5. B
6. J
7. A
8. J

Lesson 6: Titles, Introductory Elements, Direct Address
• Page 60
A. B
B. H
1. C

2. F
3. A
4. F
5. D
6. F

SAMPLE TEST
• Pages 61–64
A. G
1. B
2. H
3. A
4. F
5. D
6. G
7. D
8. G
9. D
10. F
11. B
12. H
13. B
14. F
15. D
16. H
17. C
18. G
19. A
20. H
21. B
22. H
23. D
24. F
25. B
26. F
27. D
28. G

LANGUAGE: EXPRESSION
Lesson 7: Usage
• Page 65
A. C
B. G
1. D
2. G
3. A
4. G
5. D
6. F
7. D
8. H

Lesson 8: Usage
• Page 66
A. C
B. F
1. B
2. H
3. B
4. J
5. B

Lesson 9: Usage
• Page 67
A. A
1. A
2. F
3. C
4. F

Lesson 10: Verb Tenses
• Page 68
A. A
B. H
1. A
2. J
3. B

4. G
5. C
6. J

Lesson 11: Conjunctions, Prepositions, Interjections
• Page 69
A. B
B. F
1. D
2. F
3. C
4. H
5. B
6. J

Lesson 12: Sentences
• Pages 70–71
A. A
B. G
1. B
2. H
3. A
4. G
5. D
6. H
A. C
7. D
8. F
9. A

Lesson 13: Sentences
• Page 72
A. C
1. D
2. F

Lesson 14: Paragraphs
• Page 73
A. C
1. B
2. J
3. A

Lesson 15: Paragraphs
• Page 74
A. B
1. D
2. H
3. B

Lesson 16: Paragraphs
• Page 75
A. D
1. B
2. H
3. A

Lesson 17: Paragraphs
• Page 76
A. D
1. D
2. G
3. C
4. F

SAMPLE TEST
• Pages 77–80
A. B
B. H
1. A
2. J
3. A
4. G
5. D
6. F
7. B
8. J
9. B
10. H

11. B
12. F
13. D
14. F
15. C
16. G
17. B
18. F
19. D
20. F

LANGUAGE: SPELLING
Lesson 18: Spelling Skills
• Page 81
A. A
B. G
1. D
2. G
3. A
4. G
5. C
6. H
7. B
8. J

Lesson 19: Spelling Skills
• Page 82
A. B
B. J
1. B
2. F
3. D
4. F
5. C
6. J
7. A
8. F
9. B

SAMPLE TEST
• Pages 83–84
A. D
B. G
1. A
2. J
3. B
4. H
5. C
6. F
7. D
8. F
9. C
10. H
11. A
12. J
13. B
14. H
15. A
16. G
17. C
18. J
19. A

LANGUAGE: STUDY SKILLS
Lesson 20: Study Skills
• Page 85
A. C
1. A
2. J
3. B

Lesson 21: Study Skills
• Page 86
A. C
B. G
1. D
2. G

3. C
4. J
5. C
6. J

SAMPLE TEST
• Pages 87–89
A. B
B. J
1. B
2. H
3. C
4. F
5. B
6. J
7. B
8. H
9. B
10. F
11. D
12. J
13. C
14. G
15. A
16. J

LANGUAGE PRACTICE TEST
Part 1: Language Mechanics
• Pages 92–94
A. B
1. C
2. F
3. D
4. H
5. B
6. G
7. D
8. H
9. B
10. J
11. B
12. H
13. A
14. F
15. C
16. F
17. A
18. G
19. A
20. H
21. D

Part 2: Language Expression
• Pages 95–98
A. A
1. D
2. H
3. B
4. J
5. A
6. G
7. D
8. H
9. B
10. J
11. A
12. H
13. D
14. G
15. C
16. F
17. C
18. J
19. A

Part 3: Spelling
• Pages 99–100
- A. C
- B. F
- 1. B
- 2. H
- 3. A
- 4. J
- 5. B
- 6. J
- 7. B
- 8. F
- 9. D
- 10. J
- 11. B
- 12. J
- 13. A
- 14. F
- 15. C
- 16. J
- 17. B
- 18. J
- 19. C
- 20. F

Part 4: Study Skills
• Pages 101–102
- A. D
- 1. B
- 2. F
- 3. B
- 4. F
- 5. D
- 6. H
- 7. D
- 8. H
- 9. B

MATH: CONCEPTS
Lesson 1: Numeration
• Page 103
- A. D
- B. G
- 1. D
- 2. H
- 3. B
- 4. J
- 5. A

Lesson 2: Numeration
• Page 104
- A. A
- B. J
- 1. C
- 2. F
- 3. D
- 4. F
- 5. C
- 6. G

Lesson 3: Number Concepts
• Page 105
- A. D
- B. F
- 1. C
- 2. J
- 3. B
- 4. J
- 5. C

Lesson 4: Number Concepts
• Page 106
- A. B
- B. H
- 1. C
- 2. F
- 3. C

- 4. F
- 5. D
- 6. G

Lesson 5: Properties
• Page 107
- A. D
- B. F
- 1. B
- 2. G
- 3. D
- 4. G
- 5. C

Lesson 6: Properties
• Page 108
- A. B
- B. H
- 1. D
- 2. G
- 3. C
- 4. J

Lesson 7: Place Value
• Page 109
- A. D
- B. F
- 1. D
- 2. G
- 3. B
- 4. G
- 5. B
- 6. F

Lesson 8: Fractions and Decimals
• Page 110
- A. A
- B. J
- 1. B
- 2. J
- 3. B
- 4. H

Lesson 9: Fractions and Decimals
• Page 111
- A. B
- 1. D
- 2. H
- 3. A
- 4. H
- 5. B

Lesson 10: Patterns, Expressions, Ordered Pairs
• Page 112
- A. A
- B. H
- 1. D
- 2. H
- 3. B

SAMPLE TEST
• Pages 113–114
- A. B
- B. J
- 1. C
- 2. J
- 3. A
- 4. H
- 5. C
- 6. F
- 7. B
- 8. F
- 9. C
- 10. J
- 11. C
- 12. H
- 13. A
- 14. G

- 15. A
- 16. H

MATH: COMPUTATION
Lesson 11: Addition and Subtraction of Whole Numbers
• Page 115
- A. B
- B. J
- 1. C
- 2. F
- 3. B
- 4. J
- 5. A
- 6. J
- 7. C
- 8. F

Lesson 12: Multiplication and Division of Whole Numbers
• Page 116
- A. C
- B. F
- 1. B
- 2. F
- 3. D
- 4. G
- 5. A
- 6. H
- 7. A
- 8. H

Lesson 13: Adding Fractions
• Page 117
- A. A
- 1. C
- 2. G
- 3. C
- 4. J
- 5. A
- 6. H

Lesson 14: Subtracting Fractions
• Page 118
- A. B
- B. F
- 1. A
- 2. J
- 3. C
- 4. F
- 5. B
- 6. J

Lesson 15: Multiplying and Dividing Fractions
• Pages 119–121
- A. A
- B. H
- 1. C
- 2. J
- 3. B
- 4. J
- 5. B
- 6. F
- 7. D
- 8. G
- 9. A
- 10. H
- 11. D
- 12. J
- 13. B
- 14. H
- 15. A
- 16. H
- 17. D
- 18. G
- 19. C

Lesson 16: Adding and Subtracting Decimals and Percents
• Page 122
- A. B
- B. G
- 1. C
- 2. J
- 3. A
- 4. J
- 5. C
- 6. J

Lesson 17: Multiplying and Dividing Decimals and Percents
• Page 123
- A. C
- B. F
- 1. A
- 2. G
- 3. A
- 4. H
- 5. D
- 6. G

SAMPLE TEST
• Pages 124–126
- A. C
- B. F
- 1. C
- 2. H
- 3. D
- 4. G
- 5. A
- 6. H
- 7. B
- 8. J
- 9. A
- 10. H
- 11. A
- 12. G
- 13. C
- 14. F
- 15. C
- 16. F
- 17. D
- 18. G

MATH: APPLICATIONS
Lesson 18: Geometry
• Page 126
- A. C
- 1. C
- 2. F
- 3. D
- 4. H
- 5. A
- 6. G

Lesson 19: Geometry
• Page 127
- A. B
- 1. D
- 2. F
- 3. B
- 4. J

Lesson 20: Geometry
• Page 128
- A. D
- B. H
- 1. C
- 2. H
- 3. C
- 4. J

Lesson 21: Geometry
• Page 129

- A. B
- B. H
- 1. C
- 2. J
- 3. B
- 4. H

Lesson 22: Classifying Two-Dimensional Figures
• Page 130
- A. A
- B. G
- 1. C
- 2. F
- 3. A
- 4. J
- 5. C
- 6. G

Lesson 23: Measurement
• Page 131
- A. D
- B. G
- 1. C
- 2. F
- 3. C
- 4. J

Lesson 24: Measurement
• Page 132
- A. C
- 1. B
- 2. J
- 3. C
- 4. G
- 5. D
- 6. G

Lesson 25: Measurement
• Page 133
- A. D
- B. F
- 1. D
- 2. G
- 3. A
- 4. G
- 5. C
- 6. G

Lesson 26: Measurement
• Page 134
- A. B
- B. H
- 1. B
- 2. H
- 3. D
- 4. F
- 5. B

Lesson 27: Volume
• Pages 135–136
- A. D
- B. F
- 1. C
- 2. G
- 3. D
- 4. J
- 5. D
- 6. G
- 7. B
- 8. F
- 9. D
- 10. F
- 11. C

Lesson 28: Problem Solving
• Page 137
- A. B
- 1. B

- 2. H
- 3. B
- 4. F

Lesson 29: Problem Solving
• Page 138
- A. C
- 1. C
- 2. G
- 3. D
- 4. F

Lesson 30: Problem Solving
• Page 139
- A. C
- 1. B
- 2. F
- 3. B

Lesson 31: Problem Solving
• Page 140
- A. B
- B. H
- 1. A
- 2. H
- 3. B
- 4. F

Lesson 32: Interpreting Data
• Page 141
- 1. B
- 2. F
- 3. D
- 4. J
- 5. C
- 6. H

Lesson 33: The Coordinate Plane
• Page 142
- 1. A
- 2. H
- 3. B
- 4. H
- 5. C
- 6. G

SAMPLE TEST
• Pages 143–146
- A. A
- B. G
- 1. D
- 2. H
- 3. B
- 4. F
- 5. D
- 6. H
- 7. B
- 8. F
- 9. D
- 10. H
- 11. B
- 12. J
- 13. C
- 14. J
- 15. A
- 16. H
- 17. C
- 18. J
- 19. B
- 20. F
- 21. D
- 22. F
- 23. C

MATH PRACTICE TEST
Part 1: Math Concepts
• Pages 147–148
- A. B
- B. F

1. D
2. F
3. C
4. J
5. B
6. J
7. B
8. F
9. C
10. G
11. C
12. F
13. C
14. G
15. D
16. G

Part 2: Computation
• Pages 149–150

A. B
B. F
1. D
2. G
3. A
4. J
5. B
6. H
7. C
8. F
9. D
10. G
11. C
12. J
13. C
14. J
15. C
16. F
17. C
18. G
19. D
20. H
21. B

Part 3: Math Applications
• Pages 151–154

A. A
B. J
1. B
2. J
3. B
4. G
5. D
6. G
7. C
8. G
9. D
10. H
11. C
12. F
13. D
14. F
15. C
16. G
17. D
18. G
19. A
20. H
21. D
22. F
23. B
24. J